DRINK

~ like a ~

WOMAN

DRINK
like a
WOMAN

Shake. Stir. Conquer. Repeat.

JEANETTE HURT

art by paige clark

Foreword by Ann Tuennerman
Founder of Tales of the Cocktail

SEAL PRESS

ISBN 1-58005-628-1

Library of Congress Cataloging-in-Publication Data is available.

Published by

    SEAL PRESS
    An imprint of Perseus Books
    A Hachette Book Group company
    1700 Fourth Street
    Berkeley, California
    Sealpress.com

Cover Design: Kara Davison, Faceout Studio
Interior Design: Kara Davison, Faceout Studio
Printed in China by RR Donnelley, Shenzhen

9 8 7 6 5 4 3 2 1

For Susan Ward, Bec Loss, and Jen Fichtel.
This one's for you. Cheers!

contents

1600–1900: WITCHES AND BAR WENCHES

1900–1950: VOTES FOR WOMEN, WHISKEY FOR ALL

1950–2000: LIBATIONS FOR THE LIBERATED

2000s: STIRRING UP COCKTAILS, SHAKING UP THE WORLD

PLUS!

Foreword

Damn you, Carrie Bradshaw. Damn you!

Your romp through the late 1990s and early 2000s was a never-ending conveyor belt of Cosmos and -tinis and other sugary, fruity, "girly" drinks. Would it have killed you to order a Sazerac every once in a while? Or maybe a Hanky-Panky in honor of Ada Coleman, the pioneer of female bartenders? (Jeanette will tell us more about her later.) I'm not saying *Sex and the City* created the idea of female-centric drinks, but it sure didn't do anything to lessen the stereotype that says women like only sweet, electric-colored cocktails. Really, the writers were just reflecting what was happening in the wider culture, where over-the-top drinks, premade mixers, and kitschy gimmicks ran rampant. Luckily for all of us, especially for female bartenders and bar patrons, those days are dead.

There's a reason why whiskey has moved past vodka as the number-one-selling spirit in America—and it's not just that men started drinking a lot more of it. The favorite bar call of cowboys and the manliest of men is now being enjoyed by everyone. It's no longer an anomaly to walk into a bar and see several women sipping something brown from a rocks glass. The same thing goes for all kinds of other spirits. More and more women (and men, for that matter) are now choosing their drinks based on one thing: taste. Bitter, herbaceous, fruity, spicy, sour, and, yes, even sweet. And that's the point—one that Jeanette touches on again and again throughout this book with her own brand of wit and charm. Both women and men are getting more savvy about what they want out of a cocktail, and more adventurous in what they're willing to try.

As a woman in the cocktail industry, though admittedly not on the day-to-day bartending grind, I have only experienced support. But it wasn't always that way for women in our business. There was a time in our history when we weren't even allowed *in* bars, let alone *behind* them. In fact, a 1945 Michigan law made it illegal for a woman to tend bar unless she was the wife or daughter of the bar owner. When this law was challenged in 1948 in the U.S. Supreme Court in *Goesaert v. Cleary*, the court ruled *in favor* of the Michigan law. Other laws like it stayed on the books into the 1970s.

And even after that, sexism and discrimination kept many female bartenders from being taken seriously. But then it began to change. As the cocktail revolution was bubbling up, the barrier for women started coming down. There's Audrey Saunders. Charlotte Voisey. Julie Reiner. They and so many others have helped pave the way for female bartenders, who are taking the industry by storm. In 2015, Ivy Mix was recognized as American Bartender of the Year at The Spirited Awards, part of Tales of the Cocktail, the festival that recognizes the industry's best. Not America's Best "Female" Bartender. The Best Bartender. Period. Ivy wasn't the first woman to win this honor—Saunders won in 2007. And she most definitely won't be the last, because talent is now being recognized regardless of gender.

The proof is in the glass.

No matter which side of the bar you're on—as a bartender or a customer—women have come a long way. This book is a celebration of that. Through more than fifty cocktails that cut across practically every spirit and taste profile, Jeanette honors some of history's most inspiring women. Sorry, Carrie Bradshaw, you didn't make the cut.

ANN TUENNERMAN

Founder of Tales of the Cocktail

A Word About *"Girly"* Drinks

Readers: Before you make, shake, stir, strain, blend, or muddle, let's get something straight right now. There are no "girly" drinks. There are no "manly man" drinks. There are just *drinks*, and each human has her or his own preferences—sweet, tangy, salty, spicy, sour, and so on.

Unfortunately, there are still bartenders, spirits marketers, and alcohol advertisers who assume a woman will always prefer a saccharine-sweet pink drink.

Listen up, bar butlers and hooch hawkers: Women like all kinds of bevvies. We like them big and small, strong and subtle, gussied up and straight out of the bottle. Our tastes in cocktails are as varied as our tastes in everything else.

"Women are drinking what they want to drink," says Cris Dehlavi, award-winning head bartender of M Restaurant and Pisco Porton brand ambassador. "It's often whiskey and gin and tequila, and it has nothing to do with being 'girly' at all." Julia Momose, head bartender at GreenRiver in Chicago, encourages bartenders and consumers to expand their vocabulary as wine connoisseurs do, to label drinks with more detailed terms. As Momose says, "Describe a drink as light and refreshing, or dark and stirred, or leathery or velvety or beefy."

That doesn't mean there's any shame in a woman liking sweeter drinks. It might even make some sense, scientifically. According to a study of college students in both the United States and Spain, 60 percent of the foods that both Spanish and American women craved were sweet, while 60 percent of the foods that both Spanish and American men craved were salty. Another medical study (of rats, so take this with a grain of cheese—er, salt) poses the hypothesis that females crave sweets because of the hormone estradiol. Other studies have shown that women have a greater sensitivity to bitter flavors and irritants. Women also have more taste buds than men.

Taken altogether, these studies may suggest why *some* women prefer cocktails on the sweet side. So enjoy your Mai Tais and Margaritas! Just don't call them *girly*.

Accessorizing Your Home Bar

The absolute basics you need to outfit your home bar are jiggers, a muddler, a shaker, a strainer, a bar spoon, and optional pourers. And glasses!

You also will need to borrow some equipment from your kitchen, including a sharp paring knife and cutting board, a juicer, a zester, some peelers, and a blender. (A juicer is a must when it comes to making good cocktails—fresh citrus juices are really a necessity for many classic recipes.)

You may also want an ice pick and an ice scoop. A single ice pick—the old-fashioned kind that's not too thick and not too thin—works wonders to remove the peels from all kinds of citrus. But you can also do this with a metal meat skewer or the tine of a fork—and if you twist a fork around while making a lemon twist, you can get a perfect curl. An ice scoop is ideal if you need to scoop, well, ice—but it's not necessary. What will be necessary is ice; though the recipes in this book specify ice only when it's part of the drink, as in a Daiquiri, expect to need ice for almost every drink.

In outfitting your home bar, you don't need to spend an entire paycheck, but you will want to buy durable equipment that you actually like and will use. So, let's get shaking.

JIGGERS

There are two basic types of jiggers: shot-glass jiggers and metal jiggers. Shot-glass jiggers measure two ounces; some have markings for 1.5 ounces, .75 ounce, and .5 ounce—but some don't, so you have to eyeball it. Mixing drinks is usually easier if your jiggers have partial-ounce measurements. You can also use a two-ounce measuring cup but, while it does the trick, it just doesn't look cool.

MUDDLERS

A muddler is a pestle-like tool that helps you to mash cocktail ingredients like fruit, herbs, and spices to release their flavor. You can buy a muddler designed for the task, or you can use the end of a wooden spoon or the blunt end of a butter knife.

SHAKERS

There are two basic kinds of shakers: cobbler shakers and Boston shakers.

Cobbler Shaker

The cobbler shaker is entirely metal, and it has three parts—the bottom cup, the top strainer, and the cap.

The first thing you look for in a cobbler is how it fits in your hand. Too big, and it's going to be awkward when you're shaking at your cocktail party; too small, and you won't fit the right number of drinks in it. Size does matter . . . but it's a personal thing.

The cobbler, in theory, is the easiest to use. But, depending on which cobbler you purchase, it can become your worst frenemy, as it resists your efforts to take it apart while mixing drinks at a party. Remember that a high price tag and a fancy design don't always equate to better quality. Before you buy one, be sure to ask the person selling it to you if it separates easily. Better yet, try a friend's shaker at her house first, and then, if the shaker cooperates, buy the same exact model.

Boston Shaker

The Boston shaker consists of a thick tempered mixing glass and a larger metal tumbler (the tumbler looks just like the bottom mixing cup of a cobbler). Because it doesn't have a built-in strainer, you're also going to need to purchase a strainer, called a Hawthorne strainer, which you fit over the top of the mixing glass. Mastering the Boston requires equal parts practice and patience.

To properly set up a Boston shaker, place your ingredients and ice in the mixing glass. Then set the metal tumbler on top of the mixing glass at an angle and give the bottom of it a nice, hard whack with the heel of your hand.

Once your shaker is set up, just shake, shake, shake; then, when your drink is ready, hold the shaker in one hand by placing two fingers on the mixing glass and two fingers on the metal tumbler. Using your other hand, give the shaker a good, hard whack. This is the hard part—you need to whack it in the center of the side, right where the glass and the metal seem to separate; if you hit it right, the two pieces will separate easily. But there's a knack to the whack—if you're not sure what you're doing, simply do a YouTube search for "Boston shaker" and you'll find bartenders explaining the art of the whack.

Once you separate the tumbler and the mixing glass, pour your drink into a cocktail glass of your choice, using a strainer to keep the ice in the tumbler.

STRAINERS

There are three types of strainers: Hawthorne strainers, each with a coil of metal that can be placed right into a shaker or glass; julep strainers, which are the original strainers; and tea strainers. Some bartenders like to first use either a Hawthorne or a julep and then use a tea strainer afterward.

There's a knack to using a Hawthorne strainer: place the Hawthorne strainer on the top of the metal tumbler. It has four metal tabs on top so it fits right over the tumbler, and its coiled spring ensures that it fits inside. Then use your index finger to slide the straining part of the strainer to the edge of the tumbler, and voilà! You can pour your drink.

BAR SPOONS

A good bar spoon just makes stirring stirred drinks easier. It's also the tool you use if you're layering shots. But if you don't have one, a long kitchen spoon can do in a pinch.

POURERS (OPTIONAL)

Pourers are exactly what they sound like—they're spouts you can attach to liquor bottles that allow you to pour booze more easily. They're especially helpful if you're using a jigger because they have regulators that keep the booze flowing in a steady stream.

If you don't have pourers, don't sweat it. Just be more careful when measuring your spirits, as some of them come rushing out of the bottles, which can overflow your jiggers and unbalance your drinks. For certain drinks—like the Martini—that call for dashes of bitters or other flavors, you might want to use droppers if you don't have pourers.

GLASSES

There are standard glasses used for serving most cocktails. You don't need to purchase every style of glass, but it is good to know what they all are and what they're used for.

Absinthe

These glasses are for absinthe. That's it. If you drink absinthe, you'll want this glass, and you'll also want a whole absinthe drink kit—the fancy spoon and the even fancier dispenser for dripping water through the sugar on the spoon to cloud the absinthe. If you love the Green Fairy, you'll know the equipment you need to properly consume it.

MARGARITA

CHAMPAGNE
FLUTE

MARTINI

SHOT
GLASS

HIGHBALL

Champagne

These are used for the bubbly, yes, but also for any drinks that use sparkling wine as an ingredient—Kir Royales, Bellinis, etc.

Collins, Delmonico, and Highball

Collins, Delmonico, and highball glasses are basically the same thing: chimney-style glasses, or glasses that are like taller, narrower rocks glasses. (More on rocks glasses below.) Where the three differ is in size: Delmonicos come in at five to eight ounces, highballs come in at eight to twelve ounces, and Collins glasses come in at twelve to sixteen ounces. You can use any of these glasses for Collins drinks; they're also used for liquor and mixers (Jack and Coke, whiskey and soda), Tequila Sunrises, Gin Fizzes, Gimlets, and Mojitos. You can use them for smaller-portioned Bloody Marys, too.

Cordial

Cordials are for fancy after-dinner shots—like a little taste of Frangelico.

Coupe

These glasses were originally used for Champagne and Champagne drinks, but Champagne is best served in narrow flutes so the bubbles last longer. Coupes are used now for anything frothy, like fizzes, and anything creamy, like grasshoppers; they can also be used instead of Martini glasses.

Hurricane

These glasses are great for hurricanes, tropical drinks, and Bloody Marys.

Irish Coffee

Basically, these are fancy glass mugs that are good for any coffee-based drinks, but they can also be used for straight cappuccinos. They're good for mulled wine, too.

Margarita

These glasses are made for Margaritas, of course, but they can also be used for frozen drinks.

Martini

Also known simply as cocktail glasses, Martini glasses are perfect for, well, Martinis. They're also used for Manhattans, Gimlets, creamy drinks, frothy drinks . . . anything that you serve without ice and want to keep chilled.

Poco Grande

Poco grande glasses are used for frozen and tropical drinks—your Mai Tais, piña coladas, and the like. But they can also be used for Bloody Marys, creamy dessert drinks, sangrias, and more. They are even great for serving chocolate mousse and puddings.

Pint

These glasses aren't just for ales and stouts—they're also great for Bloody Marys.

Rocks

These are the kind of cocktail glasses your grandmother might have used to mix her Southern Comfort Manhattans. They're short tumblers, and they're called "rocks," cause you usually fill them with ice. They're also known as old-fashioned glasses, named for the drink.

But besides Manhattans, you can use them to serve Martinis (on the rocks, of course), Gimlets, and after-dinner drinks like White Russians. They're also suitable for any booze that is served on the rocks.

At fancy cocktail bars, rocks glasses are typically used for drinks that are stirred, not shaken, like the old-fashioned—but they also can be used for shaken drinks not served in stemmed glasses, like mint juleps and Negronis.

Double Rocks

These are just like rocks glasses, but double the size. A regular rocks glass holds six to eight ounces of booze; a double holds twelve to fourteen ounces.

Shot

These glasses are for Jägerbombs, tequila shots, and anything your former college roommate still guzzles. But you can also use them in place of cordial glasses.

Snifter

Snifters are used for brandy, expensive whiskeys, and other booze you want to warm in your hand and sniff.

Tiki

These are great for any tropical drink. But they are also appreciated as the glass for your preschooler's milk.

Wine

Red, white, and rosé wines, of course, taste better in wine glasses, especially those made for specific varietals, but sangria and punches also can be served in wine glasses.

Don't Bust Your Budget on Bar Glasses

Before you buy a dozen or more different sets of glasses, think about what you like to drink, consider what your friends enjoy, and then buy accordingly. Depending on what you drink, you might consider buying a couple of rocks glasses, a few Martini glasses, a few highball/Collins glasses, and maybe some poco grande glasses if you especially like tropical drinks or Bloody Marys. Also, consider what glasses appeal to your sense of style—if you like Collins glasses better than rocks glasses, go ahead and serve those old-fashioneds in Collins glasses. If you prefer coupes to Martinis, then buy the coupes. No one says you can't do it. But don't bust your bank account!

Cheap but fashionable and practical glasses can be found at Goodwill stores, at estate and rummage sales, and even in your grandmother's attic. Another good bet is to go to restaurant and bar supply stores. They sell to the public, and they're cheaper than fancy home goods stores. You can also find a great selection of bar equipment there, too.

When shopping for glasses, the other thing to consider is size. Whether your glasses appear half-full or half-empty, not surprisingly, depends on their size. "A four-ounce Martini drink looks puny if you pour it into an eight-ounce glass, but it looks just right in one [for] only six ounces." So says Suzanne Bruce, bartending instructor at the College of DuPage in Glen Ellyn, Illinois.

On to the drinks!

1600–1900

Witches

AND

· BAR ·

WENCHES

Bewitched

Double, double, toil and trouble; Fire burn, and cauldron bubble.

—THE WITCHES OF
SHAKESPEARE'S *MACBETH*

While we can't say that Macbeth is exactly the *hero* of Shakespeare's play, we do know the witches are the anti-heroines. They're scorned by the men of Scotland and they don't care—they glory in their powers of prophecy and their freedom from male control.

In a modern cocktail, it's the muddle, muddle that can cause toil and trouble. While you can pretty much muddle the heck out of fruit, you can easily ruin a drink if you muddle herbs with a heavy hand. So here's a variation of a **CUCUMBER SOUTHSIDE**, a great drink with which to practice your muddle.

BEWITCHED

1½ ounces Hendrick's gin

¾ ounce fresh lemon juice

¾ ounce simple syrup (see recipe on page 201)

3 cucumber wheels

5 to 8 mint leaves

Glass: Martini or coupe

Garnish: cucumber wheel

Chill a Martini or coupe glass. Add all the ingredients to a shaker. Gently muddle—that is, press down with your muddle and twist 3 to 4 times to express the oils of the mint and the juice of the cucumbers. Add ice, and shake hard for 30 to 60 seconds. Strain into the chilled glass and garnish with a cucumber wheel.

For yet another variation on the Southside, use basil instead of mint.

Start the Revolution

Women with alcohol played a crucial role in the American Revolution. Women used alcohol to treat infections and diseases—and also served up drinks in taverns. One famous Williamsburg, Virginia, tavern owner, JANE VOBE (1765–1786), offered free food and booze to soldiers throughout the Revolution.

The most legendary woman-and-drink story is of NANCY MORGAN HART (1735–1830), a Georgia woman who dressed as a man to spy on British soldiers. When six soldiers—presumably either Tories or British enlisted men—came to her farm demanding food, she didn't just serve them dinner; she also poured her homemade corn whiskey and ensured they became inebriated. Then she removed their rifles, killed one, and wounded another.

This winning combination of whiskey and hard cider sparkles in flavor—to which we add just a kick of cinnamon syrup and bitters to give it a warm complexity. Angostura bitters work well in this recipe, but so do a variety of other bitters, including Bar Keep Baked Apple, Bittercube Blackstrap, Fee Brothers Molasses, and Fee Brothers Old Fashioned bitters. Any of these options will give this drink a nice finishing spark.

START THE REVOLUTION

¾ ounce American whiskey, preferably bourbon

¼ ounce Tuaca

¼ ounce quick cinnamon simple syrup or cinnamon simple syrup (see recipes on page 203 and 204)

1 dash Angostura bitters

3 ounces dry sparkling hard cider

Glass: 8-ounce rocks or highball

Garnish: large apple quarter, about 1 inch thick, dipped in lemon juice (to keep it from oxidizing)

Fill a rocks glass with ice. Fill a cocktail shaker with ice. Pour in the whiskey, Tuaca, cinnamon syrup, and bitters. Shake for 30 seconds. Strain the whiskey mixture into the prepared glass. Then "float" 3 ounces hard cider on top: to do this, slowly pour the cider over an inverted teaspoon (with the round side up); this technique creates an upper layer of cider. Then, to garnish, cut halfway through the apple quarter and wedge it onto the rim of the rocks glass.

How the Cocktail (Maybe) Got Its Name

Creating a new country wasn't the Revolutionary War's only subversive result. Another revolution happened behind the bar—when an American woman (might have) created the first cocktail. Though the cocktail's exact origins remain steeped in lore, one highly plausible inventor was Catharine Hustler. A tavern owner and sutler (a merchant who outfitted troops with booze), Hustler reportedly mixed up a gin concoction for soldiers during the war. Her outsized personality captivated James Fenimore Cooper, who immortalized her as tavern-keep Elizabeth "Betty" Flanagan in *The Spy: A Tale of Neutral Ground*. Today, a cocktail festival in Lewiston, New York, honors her.

Madame Magnate

MADAME CLICQUOT (1777–1866) had been married only six years when her husband died, leaving her to run the family business: Champagne. Her exceptional talent with wine was soon revealed, and she worked with her cellar master to develop a new technique of riddling, or twisting, the bottles upside down to remove the yeast.

Her title *veuve* "widow"—lives on in Veuve Clicquot luxury Champagne.

Naturally, the best cocktail to honor Madame is the classic **CHAMPAGNE COCKTAIL.**

MADAME MAGNATE

4 ounces Champagne

1 sugar cube

3 to 4 dashes Angostura bitters

Glass: Champagne flute

Garnish: lemon twist

Chill a Champagne glass. Once it's chilled, drop in a sugar cube. Add 3 to 4 dashes bitters. Top with Champagne, and garnish with a lemon twist.

note

Some versions of this cocktail include 1 ounce of cognac, added to the glass before adding the Champagne.

Jane Austen's
Zombie!

JANE AUSTEN (1775–1817) remains one of the most celebrated writers of all time. Modern authors love to pay homage to her, using her timeless novels as blueprints for modern storytelling. Her work has inspired countless revisionist tales, and her influence can be found in genres including science fiction, fantasy, political thrillers, and, of course, the killing of zombies.

Just like a zombie, Jane Austen will live forever. But the actual **ZOMBIE** drink might just wipe you out. With nearly five ounces of booze, it's about two-and-a-half drinks' worth of alcohol—but because it's so fruity, it doesn't taste like you're drinking much. Which is why several tiki bars set limits on the number of Zombies patrons can purchase.

JANE AUSTEN'S ZOMBIE!

1½ ounces El Dorado white rum

1½ ounces Myers's dark rum

1 ounce Lemon Hart 151 rum

½ ounce John D. Taylor's Velvet Falernum

½ ounce fresh grapefruit juice

2 ounces pineapple juice

¾ ounce fresh lime juice (or the juice of about half a fresh lime; save the squeezed lime, which can be used for the optional 151 fire garnish)

½ ounce cinnamon simple syrup (see recipe on page 203)

2 teaspoons grenadine (see recipe on page 206)

6 drops absinthe, preferably St. George

2 dashes Angostura bitters

Glass: tiki or poco grande

Garnish: pineapple and 1 to 2 cherries

Fill a tall tiki or poco grande glass with crushed ice. Fill a shaker with ice. Add all the ingredients and shake for 30 to 60 seconds. Strain into the prepared glass. Garnish with a slice of pineapple and a cherry or two.

For added flair, place the squeezed lime on top, fill with 1 teaspoon of 151-proof rum, and then set it on fire with a lighter or match.

note

Velvet Falernum is a Caribbean spiced liqueur made with rum and a spice-infused sugarcane syrup.

Brontë's Brew

Charlotte (*Jane Eyre*), Emily (*Wuthering Heights*), and Anne Brontë (*Agnes Grey*) published some of the greatest Victorian novels—feminist classics still celebrated generations later for their spirited heroines and their fervent discontent with patriarchal expectations of women.

Raised mostly by their aunt Elizabeth after their mother died, the Brontë sisters lived in a small parsonage where their father was pastor, and they often amused themselves by inventing and writing about fantastical worlds. The three sisters first tried their hand at poetry, which they self-published to no success whatsoever. Then they turned their pens toward novels, and their legacies were launched.

Emily, Anne, and their ne'er-do-well brother, Bramwell, all died in quick succession in 1848 and 1849, perhaps from tuberculosis. Charlotte continued writing, and she even married, but her marriage was cut short—in 1853 she died, pregnant, at the age of thirty-eight.

Their lives may have been tragically brief, but the Brontë sisters' words—and this recipe—will live on forever, inspiring the outspoken and adventurous Victorians in all of us.

Barring the Door to Women

Throughout the nineteenth century in America, bars, saloons, and taverns lived up to the title of "seedy." Spittoons with stray flecks of tobacco juice riddled the counters, and piss troughs lined the floors. Booze was almost completely unregulated, so it could be distilled by anyone with a basin in need of a quick buck—in other words, it could have been foul. Given how filthily men behaved in these establishments, they often used that behavior as justification for discrimination, banning women from being anywhere near saloons "for the protection of the delicate sex"—even if those women were trying to track down, say, their negligent husbands.

In some bars, however, women were allowed to enter—they just couldn't walk through the front doors. So, like servants denied the manor's front entrance, they used side doors, kept separate from the main action. In Wisconsin, historical Germanic taverns still boast these side entrances, which opened into small rooms that were known as ladies' parlors. Some had privacy screens to prevent women and their children from being morally corrupted by the goings-on in the main taverns. Others set up women's businesses in back, where women could shop for dresses while their hubbies drank. Women, of course, did drink in these backrooms, and some of them even smoked cigars, too. Men usually entered only if they were hawking wares or delivering booze to the ladies.

BRONTË'S BREW

1 ounce Absolut Elyx vodka

¾ ounce Pedro Ximénez sherry

1 ounce fresh lemon juice

¾ ounce Monin strawberry syrup

1 thyme sprig

Glass: copper cobbler

Garnish: mint sprig and berries, preferably strawberries

Fill a copper cobbler with ice. Fill a cocktail shaker with ice. Add all the ingredients and shake for 10 to 15 seconds. Strain the drink into the prepared copper cobbler. Garnish with a mint sprig and fresh berries.

Nellie Bly-Tai

Nellie Bly—or, rather, ELIZABETH COCHRAN (1864–1922)—was a spirited soul. She was a journalist in a time when there were hardly any women journalists, and even the other women who were reporters wrote only for the women's pages. But not Nellie—in her first gig for the *New York World,* she went undercover to expose the ill treatment of women at an insane asylum. She also famously toured the world in less than eighty days. But her very first foray into newspapers was writing a fiery rebuttal to a sexist essay that described working women as "a monstrosity," saying women were better suited to domestic duties in the home. Her passionate words earned her the job that launched her career, and we are all the better for it.

Nellie Bly has inspired women to study journalism and become writers. MAI TAIS have inspired women to enjoy cocktails. The two together make an unbeatable drink.

NELLIE BLY–TAI

1 ounce El Dorado white rum

1 ounce Myers's dark rum

1 ounce fresh lime juice

½ ounce orange curaçao

¼ ounce orgeat (see recipe on page 213)

¼ ounce simple syrup (see recipe on page 201)

Glass: tiki or poco grande

Garnish: mint sprig

Fill a tiki or poco grande glass with ice. Fill a shaker with ice. Add all the ingredients. Shake for 30 to 60 seconds, then strain into the prepared glass. Garnish with a mint sprig.

note

For an extra burst of aroma, lightly rub the mint sprig between your hands before placing it in the drink.

Tubmantini

A hard-working woman willing to risk death for freedom. An Underground Railroad conductor who led countless slaves out of the South. A spy for the Union Army who became the first woman to ever lead an army raid—and she didn't lose a single soldier.

HARRIET TUBMAN (1822–1913) was all of this and more. As she told a suffrage convention in 1896, "I was the conductor of the Underground Railroad for eight years, and I can say what most conductors can't say—I never ran my train off the track, and I never lost a passenger."

Author Glennette Tilley Turner, who wrote the children's book *An Apple for Harriet Tubman,* had the chance to talk with Harriet's grandniece, who related a story about apples. When Harriet was a girl, she was not allowed to eat apples—she was even once whipped by an overseer for eating one. But once she was free and had purchased her own home, one of the first things she planted was an apple tree—and she shared her apples with everyone who came to visit.

So a recipe to honor Harriet has to include the apple. This refreshing vodka drink uses an "apple shrub": a vinegar-sugar-fruit concoction that was once used to preserve fruit as well as to flavor drinks.

TUBMANTINI

2 ounces citrus vodka, like Sol

½ ounce honey liqueur, such as Krupnik (optional)

¾ ounce fresh apple cider

½ ounce apple shrub (recipe follows)

Glass: Martini

Garnish: apple slice

Chill a Martini glass. Fill a shaker with ice. Add all the ingredients to the shaker and shake for 30 to 60 seconds. Strain into the chilled Martini glass, then garnish with a fresh slice of apple.

note

If you prefer, you can leave out the honey liqueur. The Tubmantini without the honey liqueur has a slightly different yet still quite delicious taste.

APPLE SHRUB

1 cup grated apple
(with the peel, but without the stem and seeds)

1 cup sugar

1 cup apple cider vinegar

Place all the ingredients in a glass or plastic bowl. Stir, then cover with plastic and let sit at room temperature for 24 hours. Strain the apples using a fine mesh strainer or cheesecloth, pressing on the bits of apple to get all remaining juice.

This recipe makes about 1 cup of shrub. You can use it in the Tubmantini, or you can combine 1 to 2 ounces of shrub with 3 to 5 ounces of club soda or seltzer for a refreshing, grown-up soda. You can also use it in place of vinegar in vinaigrette recipes.

Monthly Medicinal

By the 1830s, an American man drank an average of seven gallons of pure alcohol every year, or the equivalent of ninety bottles of 80-proof booze. Women, for their part, as they weren't yet allowed in saloons, got their fix with concoctions like "women's tonics," pioneered by feminist abolitionist Lydia Pinkham to ease menstrual symptoms.

Give this version a try—and don't be surprised when it relieves what ails you.

MONTHLY MEDICINAL

1 ounce PAMA pomegranate liqueur

1 ounce Elijah Craig small batch bourbon

2 ounces freshly brewed and cooled hibiscus tea

½ ounce fresh lemon juice

½ ounce simple syrup (see recipe on page 201)

Glass: Collins

Garnish: lemon twist and hibiscus flower

Combine all the ingredients in a shaker, add Ice, and shake until well chilled. Fill a Collins glass with fresh ice and strain the cocktail into the glass. Garnish with a lemon twist and a hibiscus flower.

Curie Royale

MADAME MARIE CURIE (1867–1934), born Marya Skłodowska, remains one of the most celebrated scientists of all time. Not only did she discover radium and polonium; she was also the first woman ever awarded a Nobel Prize: in 1903, for physics. She was also the first scientist of either gender to win two Nobel Prizes, earning her second one for chemistry in 1911.

Still queen of firsts, Curie was the first female professor at the Sorbonne. She later passed on her passion for potions to her daughter, Irène Joliot-Curie—who followed in her footsteps and won the Nobel Prize in chemistry in 1935—and her granddaughter, who became a nuclear physicist.

"Life is not easy for any of us," Madame Curie once said. "But what of that? We must have perseverance and above all confidence in ourselves. We must believe that we are gifted for something and that this thing must be attained."

What sort of cocktail could honor such a brilliant mind? Well, one that sparkles, naturally. The Curie Royale is based on the **KIR ROYALE**. A simple Kir is crème de cassis topped with white wine; a Kir Royale is topped with Champagne. This recipe instead uses sparkling cider and Chambord.

CURIE ROYALE

1 ounce Chambord raspberry liqueur
4 ounces sparkling cider
Glass: Champagne flute
Garnish: apple sliver and/or raspberry

Pour the Chambord into a Champagne flute. Top with the sparkling cider. Garnish with a raspberry and/or apple sliver.

— *Ada's* —
Hanky Panky

A barmaid in the nineteenth century wasn't exactly celebrated in jolly old England, but she fared well enough. The Victorian era (1837–1901) was a period of cultural expansion, including in regard to women and alcohol. Unfortunately, that loosening of strict standards also meant more women bore the negative effects of alcohol—especially too much of it. But for the most part, women found their way around a barstool just fine.

It was during this time that the first celebrity female mixologists rose to prominence. ADA COLEMAN (1875–1966) started her career at the bar at Claridge's, a luxury hotel, in 1899. She was so popular that she was then moved to The Savoy and elevated to head bartender. Ada's popularity stemmed from the fact that she had both the creativity for new cocktails and the charm to serve them with panache. She and another 'tender at The Savoy, Ruth Burgess, were dubbed "Kitty and Coley" by the London press. In all, the two served a veritable who's who of celebrities, including Mark Twain, the Prince of Wales, and actor/director Sir Charles Henry Hawtrey.

Sir Charles, a stage and silent film actor, was one of Ada's regulars—and it was his dramatic reaction to one of her libations that led to its naming. After asking for a drink with a bit of "punch," Ada mixed together a memorable meld of gin, sweet vermouth, and just a touch of Fernet-Branca. Sir Charles chugged the drink, exclaiming, "By Jove! That is the real Hanky Panky!" Today, HANKY PANKY cocktails are served and sipped across the globe.

The Savoy Hotel's American Bar remains a celebrated cocktail institution. Coley is the only female head bartender to have served there, where the Hanky Panky remains on the menu.

ADA'S HANKY PANKY

¾ ounce London dry gin

¾ ounce sweet vermouth

1 to 2 dashes Fernet-Branca

Glass: Martini

Garnish: orange twist

Fill a large mixing glass with ice. Pour in the gin, vermouth, and Fernet-Branca. Stir until combined, then strain into a Martini glass. Rub the orange peel around the rim of the glass, squeeze the peel over the cocktail, and drop it in the glass as an aromatic garnish.

note

Fernet-Branca is an Italian bitter liqueur made with twenty-seven different herbs and spices. It's classified as an *amaro*, and it's often served up neat, as a digestif (an after-dinner drink believed to help the body digest a meal). It's also sometimes mixed with equal parts of Coca-Cola.

variations

Most Hanky Panky recipes call for equal parts gin and sweet vermouth, with just a dash or two of Fernet-Branca. Some recipes swear by the addition of a dash or two of orange bitters and/or 1½ teaspoons of freshly squeezed orange juice. Try the original recipe first, then embellish to your taste.

Amelia Takes Flight

—————◆—————

Most of us know that AMELIA EARHART (1897–1937) was the first woman to fly solo across the Atlantic Ocean, and that she disappeared during her attempt to be the first woman to fly around the world.

But what many may not know but which might not surprise is that, as a girl, she climbed trees, hunted rats with a .22 rifle, and kept an inspiring scrapbook of newspaper clippings about women in predominantly male-oriented fields. She also set numerous other flying records: she was the first person to fly solo across the Pacific, she broke the women's altitude record in 1922, and she was the first person to fly solo nonstop from Mexico City to Newark, New Jersey.

And what better drink to commemorate this adventurer than the classic **AVIATION** cocktail? The Aviation blends gin with maraschino and crème de violette liqueurs and lemon juice. It's a sweet, violet-blue-hued beauty. Different recipes for the Aviation abound, usually regarding the ratios of maraschino liqueur to crème de violette. The recipe here calls for a 3:1 ratio, but some other recipes call for equal parts of both liqueurs. The more violette liqueur you add, the more violet the drink becomes—and the sweeter it tastes.

AMELIA TAKES FLIGHT

2 ounces gin

¾ ounce maraschino liqueur

¼ ounce crème de violette

¾ ounce fresh lemon juice

Glass: Martini or coupe

Garnish: cherry or edible flower

Fill a shaker with ice. Add all the ingredients and shake for 30 to 60 seconds. If garnishing with a cherry, put it in the bottom of the Martini or coupe glass before straining the mix into it. Otherwise, strain the mixture into a glass, and float an edible flower atop the cocktail.

1900–1950

VOTES
for
WOMEN
Whiskey
FOR ALL

Moonshine Mama

The year 1920 was a momentous one for the States: on January 17, the country went "dry," as the prohibition on alcohol went into effect; and on August 18, women were finally granted the right to vote—after forty-one years of campaigning.

From this time forward, newspapers adored publishing stories and exposés on any women who engaged in boozy enterprises. Arrests of moonshine-making mamas made the front page, and famous female bootleggers were frequently stalked by the paparazzi of the day. One of the most infamous rum-running royals was GERTRUDE "CLEO" LYTHGOE, a.k.a. "Queen of the Bahamas" (1888–1974), who legally exported liquor for a London firm in the Bahamas before realizing the real money was in bootlegging. Packing both a pistol and an attitude, she made headlines around the country. She eventually retired after being charged with—though never convicted of—smuggling in New Orleans.

To honor Gertie's rum-running roguery, we present a version of PLANTER'S PUNCH. Some versions of this drink use just lemon and/or lime juice, but we prefer the orange-and-lemon blend.

MOONSHINE MAMA

1 ounce dark rum

1½ ounces orange juice

¼ ounce fresh lemon juice

¼ ounce simple syrup (see recipe on page 201)

¼ ounce grenadine (see recipe on page 206)

dash orange bitters

Glass: tiki or Collins

Garnish: half-moon orange slice and (maraschino) cherry "flag"

Fill a glass with ice. Fill a shaker with ice. Add all the ingredients and shake for at least 1 minute. Strain into the glass. To make the orange "flag" garnish, wrap a half-moon orange slice around a cherry or maraschino cherry, then secure it with a toothpick or cocktail umbrella.

variation

For a boozier version, add ¼ ounce Cointreau and an additional ¼ ounce simple syrup.

Suzy B's Virgin Voter

SUSAN B. ANTHONY (1820–1906) may have been a firm believer in temperance, but she still deserves a party. She fought the good fight against slavery, and led the charge for women to be granted the right to vote and own property.

A cocktail doesn't need to contain alcohol to be tasty. Here's a light and refreshing mocktail to celebrate Suzy B.

SUZY B'S VIRGIN VOTER

½ cup cranberry juice (100 percent juice blend)

1 tablespoon honey

1 teaspoon fresh lime juice

4 to 6 drops lime essential oil (see note, next page)

½ cup seltzer water or club soda

Glass: any will do

Garnish: 1 lime twist or wedge and 4 to 5 fresh cranberries

Fill the serving glass with ice. Then, in a large mixing glass, add the cranberry juice, honey, lime juice, and 2 to 3 drops lime essential oil and stir until combined. Pour into the prepared serving glass, then top off with seltzer water. For a garnish, rub the lime twist or wedge around the glass before dropping it in the drink. Drizzle the remaining 2 to 3 drops lime essential oil over the cocktail, and drop in fresh cranberries to finish.

(continued on next page)

SUZY B'S VIRGIN VOTER

note

You need to be sure that the lime essential oil you use is meant for human consumption (DoTerra and Young Living oils are two possibilities). If you can't find food-grade oil, then add an additional ½ teaspoon lime juice just before serving to produce a greater lime aroma.

variation

To transform this Virgin Voter into a Fiery Suffragist, add 1½ ounces vodka, rum, tequila, or gin in the initial measuring of the ingredients.

Of Spirits and Suffrage

For women in the nineteenth and early twentieth centuries, the right to vote and the temperance movement were linked. While women sought the vote for a singular reason, women campaigned for temperance for many reasons. Prime among them: men who drank too much, squandered family funds, abused women and children, and generally behaved quite badly.

"The temperance movement was about women slowly growing an awareness, getting a sense of having power over their own destinies," says Michelle Gullion, archives director and curator for the National First Ladies Library. "Women had no rights, and if you were a woman, you were basically property."

Interestingly, it was her support of temperance that led Susan B. Anthony (1820–1906), one of the leaders of the suffrage movement, to get involved in women's rights. Born to a Quaker family who considered drinking sinful, Anthony joined the Daughters of Temperance, eventually becoming president of the Rochester, New York, branch. She later joined with Elizabeth Cady Stanton and founded the Women's State Temperance Society. Their goal: for the New York state legislature to limit the sale of alcohol. Why they failed: legislators rejected their petition because most of the signatures were from women and children. From this, Anthony realized women needed the right to have a voice in political affairs before they could effect change with that voice.

Flapper's Firewater

Prohibition, which lasted until 1933, fueled the Jazz Age, when music went wild and speakeasies turned a blind eye to the Eighteenth Amendment. Women, newly empowered with the right to vote, won in 1920—joined men at the speakeasies which replaced saloons. With bobbed hair and red lips, swinging to the beat of the Charleston and the Black Bottom, they daringly smoked cigarettes and drank cocktails in public.

In honor of this historic development, shake some fine bourbon with cranberry liqueur and Meletti 1870 bitter liqueur.

Meet You in the Powder Room

As flappers flocked to nightclubs in greater numbers than ever before, owners needed to find bathroom facilities for their new customers. Broom closets and other tucked-away places were converted into bathrooms, but the tiny spaces could not accommodate more than a sink, a mirror, and a toilet. Voilà: the birth of the "powder room."

FLAPPER'S FIREWATER

1½ ounces bourbon

½ ounce Clear Creek cranberry liqueur

½ ounce Meletti 1870 Bitter liqueur

¼ ounce lemon juice

¼ ounce honey simple syrup (see recipe on page 208 and omit the rosemary)

3 drops rosewater

Glass: coupe

Garnish: rose petal

Fill a cocktail shaker with ice, and add all ingredients. Shake for 60 seconds. Strain into a coupe glass and garnish with a rose petal.

*The Flapper awoke from
her lethargy of sub-deb-ism,
bobbed her hair, put on her
choicest pair of earrings and a
great deal of audacity and rouge
and went into the battle. She
flirted because it was fun to flirt
and wore a one-piece bathing suit
because she had a good figure, she
covered her face with powder and
paint because she didn't need it,
and she refused to be bored chiefly
because she wasn't boring.*

—ZELDA FITZGERALD

from "Eulogy on the Flapper"

Zeldapolitan

ZELDA FITZGERALD (1900–1948) was more than just a famous flapper—she also embodied the zeitgeist of womanpower during the Roaring Twenties. A writer, painter, and socialite, she was famously married to F. Scott Fitzgerald. At times both passionate and pained, Zelda inspired some of Fitzgerald's most celebrated works to such an extent that literary historians believe he very likely lifted passages right out of her diaries.

With what to toast Zelda? Why, a riff on the **COSMOPOLITAN**, of course.

The basic **COSMO** calls for 1½ ounces citrus vodka, 1 ounce orange liqueur (triple sec or Cointreau are the most popular), ½ ounce Rose's lime juice (or ¼ ounce fresh lime juice and ¼ ounce simple syrup), plus 1 to 2 dashes (about ½ ounce) cranberry juice, garnished with a lemon twist and served in a Martini glass.

Because Zelda was more likely to drink gin instead of vodka, the Zeldapolitan is similar to a Cosmo but with a daring twist, just like the woman herself.

ZELDAPOLITAN

1½ ounces gin

½ ounce cranberry juice (100 percent juice blend)

½ ounce fresh lime juice

½ ounce simple syrup (see recipe on page 201)

2 dashes citrus bitters

Glass: Martini

Garnish: lime twist

Fill a shaker with ice. Pour in all the ingredients and shake for about 30 seconds or until well chilled. Strain into a Martini glass and garnish with a twist of lime.

Grace Under
Pressure

LADY GRACE DRUMMOND-HAY (1895–1946) was a celebrated British journalist; she also was the first woman to travel around the world by air. She did this in 1929 in a zeppelin (a blimp-like rigid airship, such as the LZ 129 *Hindenburg*). The trip took twenty-nine days, and Lady Grace was the only female passenger.

Lady Grace went on to cover war zones in Africa and China. Unfortunately, during World War II she was interned in a Japanese prisoner-of-war camp in the Philippines, where she grew terribly ill. She died not long after the war ended, succumbing to a weakened heart at the age of fifty.

But her adventurous spirit lives on—as does the dirigible. The folks at Hendrick's, whose gin is infused with cucumbers, came up with this tasty cocktail to celebrate their giant cucumber-shaped dirigible, which accepted its first passengers in April 2015.

GRACE UNDER PRESSURE

1½ ounces Hendrick's gin

1 ounce Chardonnay

1½ teaspoons citric acid

1¼ teaspoons simple syrup (see recipe on page 201)

1 dash orange bitters

Glass: Martini (or metal flask)

Fill a glass or metal shaker with ice. Add all the ingredients and stir to chill. Strain into a Martini glass—unless, of course, you happen to be riding in *The Flying Cucumber*. If so, then strain the cocktail into a flask to enjoy at an altitude of five hundred feet.

Out of the Sidecar

Motorcycle sidecars were invented so that the motorcycle driver could safely transport an extra passenger or load. Very often, women rode in sidecars.

But women didn't only tag along when men were driving. One of the most fantastic journeys involving a motorcycle and a sidecar was completed by the daughter-mother duo of Effie and Avis Hotchkiss. In 1915, Effie drove her motorcycle, with her mother in the sidecar, from Brooklyn, New York, to San Francisco, California, and back again, making them the first women to ride across the country on a motorcycle.

The classic **SIDECAR** originally started out as equal parts brandy or cognac, orange liqueur, and lemon juice; but most modern bartenders make it with two parts brandy or cognac to one part each of orange liqueur and lemon juice. It's a tart yet slightly sweet cocktail, best served in a Martini or coupe glass that's been dipped in lemon juice and then rubbed in sugar.

OUT OF THE SIDECAR

1 tablespoon extra-fine sugar

1 lemon wedge

1½ ounces cognac or brandy

¾ ounce Cointreau or other orange liqueur

¾ ounce fresh lemon juice

¼ to ½ ounce of simple syrup or oleo saccharum (optional; see note, next page)

Glass: Martini or coupe

Garnish: lemon twist, orange peel, or cherry

First, prepare the glass. Pour the sugar onto a small plate. Wipe the lemon wedge, juice side down, around the edge of a Martini or coupe glass. Twirl the lemon-rimmed glass into the sugar to create a sugared rim.

Then, fill a shaker with ice. Add cognac or brandy, Cointreau or orange liqueur, lemon juice, and simple syrup or oleo saccharum. Shake for at least 30 seconds. Strain into the prepared glass, then garnish with a lemon twist, orange peel, or cherry.

note

If this recipe is too tart for your liking, you can add an additional ¼ to ½ ounce simple syrup or oleo saccharum. (Cocktail & Sons bottles a great, handcrafted oleo saccharum, or see the recipe on page 212 to make it yourself.)

Invasion of Women

Prohibition was officially repealed on December 5, 1933. While its demise was celebrated far and wide, there were some (men) who were put out that women continued to patronize drinking joints after repeal. Don Marquis, a columnist for both the *New York Sun* and the *Saturday Evening Post*, was so miffed that he wrote a book in protest. *Her Foot Is on the Brass Rail*, published in 1935, decried the downfall of the "Old Barroom," whining that men-only bars were "gone forever, killed by this invasion of women."

"What we had wanted," complained Don, "what we had hoped and prayed for, what we had fought, bled, died and lied for, was the return of the Old Barroom . . . Women come into this New Barroom. Not through a Family Entrance, but through the front door. They go right up to the bar. They put a foot on the brass railing. They order; they are served; they bend the elbow; they hoist; they toss down the feminine esophagus the brew that was really meant for men."

Here's a twist on the DAIQUIRI, which you can drink with your own "feminine esophagus."

INVASION OF WOMEN

2 ounces rum

1 ounce fresh lime juice

½ to ¾ ounce (or more) simple syrup (see recipe on page 201), to taste

Glass: coupe or Martini

Garnish: lime wheel or wedge

Chill a coupe or Martini glass. Fill a shaker with ice, and add the rum, lime juice, and ½ ounce simple syrup. Shake for 30 seconds or until chilled and blended. Possibly add more simple syrup, to taste. Once you are satisfied with the flavor, strain the mix into the chilled glass and garnish with a lime wheel or wedge.

note

The sweetness or tartness of this drink depends on both the lime juice and the rum(s) you use. Add just ½ ounce simple syrup to start, and let your taste buds decide if you should add more.

(continued on next page)

INVASION OF WOMEN

another variation

You could also use oleo saccharum instead of simple syrup. Oleo saccharum is basically a citrus cordial, made with lime or lemon peels and sugar to extract the citrus oils. You can buy the excellent handcrafted Cocktail & Sons oleo saccharum or even make it yourself (see recipe on page 212).

For a Hemingway Daiquiri, add ¼ ounce maraschino liqueur, ¼ ounce freshly squeezed grapefruit juice, and a few drops of citrus bitters to the shaker. You can even try using a combination of homemade grapefruit and lime bitters. (You can find recipes in Brad Thomas Parsons's book *Bitters: A Spirited History of a Classic Cure-All, with Cocktails, Recipes, and Formulas*.)

Waitress Warfare

When Prohibition ended in 1933, male waiters and bartenders suddenly found their moral high horses when they realized they might lose their jobs to women. And so the Hotel and Restaurant Employees and Bartenders International Union called for completely restricting women from serving alcohol—since it would "morally corrupt" them.

Waitresses' unions fought back; by 1936, many unions had finally accepted that waitresses should be allowed to work in places that sold liquor. But this agreement often came with stipulations, like requiring that such establishments also serve food, and not allowing women behind the bar. Some waitress unions prohibited members from even garnishing a drink.

According to Professor Dorothy Sue Cobble, author of *Dishing It Out: Waitresses and Their Unions in the Twentieth Century*, these working-class waitresses were concerned that pushing for the right to work behind the bar could prevent them from working at any booze-serving establishments. In her book, Cobble calls the profession of bartending "the closed priesthood."

Clementine's Coffee

CLEMENTINE PADDLEFORD (1898–1967), a food writer for the *New York Herald Tribune*, traversed the globe in search of culinary gems. She discovered the delights of Irish coffee at the Foynes (now Shannon) Airport. In her story about this discovery, she thanked Pan American World Airways ground hostess Maureen Grogan for tracking down the recipe for her. "Sip, and the whiskey laces through the coffee, through cream," Clementine wrote. Her story and recipe for Irish coffee were published on St. Patty's Day in 1948.

A daring adventure-seeker whom *The New York Times* described as the "Nellie Bly of culinary journalism," Clementine also boasted her own private-plane license—with which she often jetted herself in search of novel tastes. In her memoir, *A Flower for My Mother*, she shared her mother's wisdom: "Never grow a wishbone, daughter, where your backbone ought to be."

For Clementine, here's an IRISH COFFEE.

CLEMENTINE'S COFFEE

1½ ounces Irish whiskey

4 to 6 ounces hot coffee

2 to 4 tablespoons sweetened whipped heavy cream

Glass: really fun mug

Garnish: green crème de menthe (optional)

Pour the Irish whiskey in your fun mug. Add coffee, leaving at least ½ inch of space at the top. Top with 2 to 4 tablespoons of sweetened whipped heavy cream. Garnish, if desired, with a few drops of green crème de menthe.

variations

Instead of Irish whiskey, you can substitute an Irish cream liqueur, like Baileys, or you can use chocolate, mint, vanilla, or caramel liqueur, or Frangelico or amaretto . . . basically any flavor that goes well with coffee. If you use two liqueurs, measure ¾ ounce of each.

DÑA Colada

As a girl, Brit ROSALIND FRANKLIN (1920–1958) was discouraged by her father from following her passion for the sciences. But Rosalind persevered, becoming a brilliant chemist and X-ray crystallographer. Then, when her photos of DNA revealed a key to uncovering its structure, she forever changed medical history.

Not that she was credited for it. Rosalind and her colleague, Maurice Wilkins, both worked on DNA at a lab at King's College in London, but they worked on separate projects. According to the San Diego Supercomputer Center—which has a computer named after Rosalind—Maurice treated Rosalind as an assistant instead of as a peer scientist.

While Maurice's treatment of Rosalind was egregious, he did worse behind her back. Unbeknownst to her, Maurice shared her photographs with rival investigators James Watson and Francis Crick; the three men then used her research to publish their own conclusions in *Nature* magazine. Though Rosalind's work was published as a supporting article in the same journal, it was that male trio who received a 1962 Nobel Prize, not Rosalind.

Just as science was in Rosalind's DNA, the **PIÑA COLADA** is in the DNA of all tropical drinks.

DÑA COLADA

2 to 3 ounces dark rum (such as Myers's), plus ½ ounce for float

¼ cup canned pineapple

¼ cup coconut cream

1½ cups ice

½ teaspoon ground nutmeg

Glass: poco grande, tiki, or other exotic glass

Garnish: ground nutmeg

Pour the rum, pineapple, and coconut cream into a blender. Add the ice and ½ teaspoon nutmeg. Blend until frothy. Pour into a poco grande, tiki, or exotic glass. Then, "float" ½ ounce dark rum on top: to do this, slowly pour the rum over an inverted teaspoon (with the round side up); this technique creates an upper layer of rum. Finish with a sprinkle of ground nutmeg.

Dottie Collins

When professional baseball players were called up to serve in World War II, Chicago Cubs owner Philip K. Wrigley cooked up a plan to keep the fans coming out to the ballparks. He created an All-American Girls Professional Baseball League, with four teams and sixty players recruited from all over the United States and Canada.

Pitcher DOROTHY "DOTTIE" COLLINS (1923–2008) led the league; she had more strikeouts than any other player, and an earned-run average of just 0.83. In 1945 she threw two no-hitters and seventeen shutouts, earning the moniker "Strikeout Queen." With an arm like a gun and a wit to match, she pitched, batted, and ran the bases for six years—only retiring her uniform when she entered her fourth month of pregnancy.

The traditional TOM COLLINS recipe combines gin with sweet and sour, and is topped with fizzy soda. But instead of gin you can use rum, brandy, whiskey . . . any liquor or liqueur.

An especially delicious Dottie Collins can be made with Tuaca instead of gin—Tuaca is an Italian liqueur flavored with vanilla and citrus.

DOTTIE COLLINS

1½ ounces gin, or another liquor or liqueur

1 ounce simple syrup (see recipe on page 201)

1 ounce fresh lemon juice

1 ounce club soda

Glass: Collins (of course!)

Garnish: half-moon orange slice and
(maraschino) cherry "flag"

Fill a Collins glass with ice. Fill a shaker with ice. Add your liquor/liqueur of choice, simple syrup, and lemon juice. Shake for 5 to 10 seconds. Strain into the prepared glass and top with the club soda. To make the orange "flag" garnish, wrap a half-moon orange slice around a cherry or maraschino cherry, then secure it with a toothpick or cocktail umbrella.

White Mouse

NANCY WAKE (1912–2011) was a World War II renegade and hero. A leading figure of the French resistance, she was the Allies' most decorated servicewoman, and a recipient of the U.S. Presidential Medal of Freedom. But when she wasn't saving the world, she sipped cocktails at the American Bar at the Stafford Hotel in London, where she lived for two years. On most days she enjoyed a gin and tonic at her own place at the bar, which manager Benoit "Ben" Provost called "Nancy's Corner."

If you go to the American Bar today, you'll find a still-reserved barstool for Nancy. Ben was so taken with her charm and courage that he has honored her with a cocktail called the "WHITE MOUSE"—what the Nazis called her; they could corner her, but they could never catch her. Death itself couldn't catch her for nearly a century; she lived to the ripe age of ninety-eight.

WHITE MOUSE

1 ounce Saffron gin
½ ounce fresh lemon juice
½ ounce honey
1 to 2 ounces Champagne
Glass: coupe glass
Garnish: whole star anise

Fill a shaker with ice. Add the gin, lemon juice, and honey. Shake for 30 to 60 seconds, then strain into a coupe glass. Top with Champagne. Garnish with star anise.

I wish to live to 150 years old, but the day I die,
I wish it to be with a cigarette in one hand and a
glass of whiskey in the other.

—AVA GARDNER

Rosé the Riveter

After working those machines, building those ships, and doing anything else that needed doing, ROSIE THE RIVETER earned the right to unwind with a wine cocktail.

ROSÉ THE RIVETER

2 ounces Hangar 1 straight vodka

1 ounce rosé wine

1 teaspoon elderflower syrup

1 teaspoon rose water

½ ounce fresh lemon juice

4 ounces seltzer water or club soda

Glass: Collins

Garnish: lemon wheel

In a glass filled with ice, pour vodka, rosé wine, elderflower syrup, rose water, and lemon juice. Stir until chilled. Top with seltzer water or club soda. Garnish with a lemon wheel.

note

Elderflower syrup (a blossom-flavored sugar syrup) and rose water (a rose-scented infusion) can be found in gourmet grocery stores and online shops.

Bessie's Game Changer

In the "Waitress Warfare" sidebar (see page 83) we saw that, though waitress unions in the 1930s successfully secured the right to work in booze-selling establishments, they were nonetheless often barred from even garnishing a drink. In the decade following, when Bubba the bartender went off to fight in WWII, Bessie took over behind the mahogany. And though the unions did allow them membership, they did so mainly to ensure the bartending positions were still occupied by union members.

Union membership grew—and so did the numbers of female bartenders, often referred to as "barmaids." By 1945, for example, there were one thousand women mixing drinks in New York City alone.

But that height was achieved in the same year the war ended— and with it ended that union support. As soon as returning war veterans wanted their jobs back, union organizers reupped their campaign against women with a vengeance.

The greatest such vehemence came from Hugo Ernst, the union's acting president in 1946. He wrote: "Few, indeed, are the number of women physically and temperamentally qualified to endure the hardships connected with tending bar. Let's all co-operate in an effort to put into effect again the traditional principle of our International Union that bartending is a man's job!"

Well, we know differently. We also know that advances for women have often taken the pace of two steps forward, one step back. So, to celebrate the slow but steady march forward, we offer Bessie's Game Changer. Named after BESSIE THE BARTENDER—as Rosie the Riveter's counterpart behind the bar is often called—this cocktail is modeled on the classic GIN FIZZ, but updated with a floral twist.

A proper Gin Fizz needs to be really, really shaken hard to get that nice, frothy finish. Anytime you add egg white to a cocktail—which doesn't add flavor, just texture—you need to shake it, and then shake it, and then shake it some more. As one bartender described, "First I shake it with my right hand until it gets tired, and then I shake it with my left hand until it gets tired." (Note that many consider the chances of getting salmonella bacteria from raw eggs to be extremely minimal; note too that few bartenders consider powdered egg white substitutes palatable in drinks.)

BESSIE'S GAME CHANGER

2 ounces North Shore Distiller's Gin No. 6

½ ounce fresh lemon juice

¾ ounce lavender-infused simple syrup
(see recipe on page 209)

1 ounce egg white (or egg white from 1 large egg)

2 to 3 ounces club soda

Glass: Collins

Garnish: lemon curl

Pour the gin, lemon juice, lavender-infused simple
syrup, and egg white into a cocktail shaker. Shake
this mixture without ice for about 1 minute. Then fill
with ice and shake, shake, shake—*hard*—for 1 to 2
minutes. Strain into a chilled Collins glass and top
with 2 to 3 ounces club soda. Garnish with a curl
of lemon.

Dorothy Parker

Apropos, Dorothy Parker has a gin honoring her legacy. The New
York Distilling Company, owned by Samantha Katz and her husband,
Allen, makes a delicious Dorothy Parker gin.   ➡

I like to have a martini,
Two at the very most.
After three I'm under the table,
after four I'm under my host.

—DOROTHY PARKER

Felix Fixer

In rendering the majority opinion of a six-to-three vote upholding a discriminatory law against women bartenders in Michigan in 1948, U.S. Supreme Court JUSTICE FELIX FRANKFURTER wrote: "Michigan evidently believes that the oversight assured through ownership of a bar by a barmaid's husband or father minimizes the hazards that may confront a barmaid without such protective oversight. . . . We cannot give ear to the suggestion that the real impulse behind this legislation was an unchivalrous desire of male bartenders to try to monopolize the calling."

One saving grace: three justices dissented, saying, "The statute arbitrarily discriminates between male and female owners of liquor establishments." But the majority set the precedent, and in time twenty-six states passed laws against women tending bar.

These laws didn't begin to change until more than two decades later. Though we can't go back in time to denounce Felix's chauvinism—as well as the chauvinism of the five other majority justices—we can offer a quaffing drink to drown such sorrows.

FELIX FIXER

½ ounce hibiscus-infused reposado tequila
(see note below)

¾ ounce oleo saccharum (see recipe on page 212)

½ ounce fresh lime juice

4 drops homemade habanero shrub tincture or
Bittermens Hellfire Habanero Shrub

black pepper

Glass: coupe

Garnish: lime wheel

Fill a shaker with ice. Add the tequila, oleo saccharum, lime juice, and habanero shrub. Add
the black pepper: either two shakes of a pepper
shaker or two twists of a pepper mill. Shake for
30 to 60 seconds. Double-strain into a coupe
glass and garnish with a lime wheel.

note

To infuse the tequila, put 6 ounces of tequila with
1½ teaspoons dried hibiscus flowers in a glass jar or
bottle. Let this sit for at least 2 hours, then strain.

Dirty Helen

HELEN CROMWELL (1886–1969) was a madam, a tavern keeper, and a buddy of Al Capone.

Helen had a mouth on her that made sailors blush, earning her the nickname "Dirty Helen," and she served only two drinks in her Milwaukee bar, The Sunflower Inn: Old Fitzgerald bourbon and House of Lords scotch. And if you asked for mixers, ice, or even a chair to sit on, you'd be laughed out of the joint. But while Helen firmly believed that if you weren't drinking scotch or bourbon, you shouldn't be drinking, she liked a lot of people, was a friend to those in both low and high places, and never lost her sense of humor.

Meanwhile, another Helen, Helen David, and her mother, Elizabeth Hibye, quietly defied Michigan law to run the Brass Rail in Port Huron. When Elizabeth first converted the family ice cream parlor into a tavern in 1937, Helen told her, "Proper ladies do not run a saloon." Elizabeth's rejoinder: "A lady is a lady no matter where you put her, but she's got to have a buck in her pocket."

Helen came around and mentored generations of bartenders, and the Tales of the Cocktail festival honors acclaimed mixologists with the Helen David Lifetime Achievement Award.

To toast either Helen properly, pour yourself a glass of bourbon or scotch and be done with it. Or you can try this gussied-up cocktail in her honor. She likely would've cussed you out for drinking it, but it's still fun to make.

DIRTY HELEN

1¼ ounces bourbon

¾ ounce maraschino liqueur

1 dash orange bitters

Glass: rocks

Garnish: none

In a glass filled with ice, stir together bourbon and maraschino liqueur. Strain into a plain rocks glass, add a dash of bitters, and serve. If you wish to get fancy, serve this over crushed ice, and then fill the glass to the top with club soda.

Frida Kahlúa

———◇———

Brilliant, tempestuous, and wildly creative, FRIDA KAHLO (1907–1954) was one of the most admired woman painters in the world. She was also prolific, despite—or maybe because of—the pain she endured, from the time she was a teenager, from a horrific injury in a trolley accident. Her vibrant work explored many taboo subjects, including gender inequality, female sexuality, infertility, lesbianism, and repressive beauty ideals.

In addition to her artistic work, she was known for her passionate, tempestuous marriage to muralist Diego Rivera. Over their two-plus decades together, both Frida and Diego seemed to fall in and out of love with each other—and with other people, too. "There have been two great accidents in my life," Frida said. "One was the trolley, and the other was Diego. Diego was far worse."

Hot and strong, the MEXICAN COFFEE is the perfect drink to honor this groundbreaking artist.

FRIDA KAHLÚA

1½ ounces Kahlúa or other coffee liqueur

4 to 6 ounces coffee

Glass: coffee mug or cup

Garnish: sweetened whipped cream and chocolate-covered coffee beans

Pour the Kahlúa into the coffee mug or cup. Add coffee, leaving at least ½ inch of space at the top. Top with 2 to 4 tablespoons of sweetened whipped heavy cream. Garnish with a couple chocolate-covered coffee beans.

Texas Twist

MARY LOUISE CECILIA "TEXAS" GUINAN (1884–1933) was a vaudevillian actress and chorus girl who in 1917 broke into film, making her the first on-screen cowgirl, for which she was named "Queen of the West." During Prohibition, she opened up a little speakeasy called the 300 Club in New York City, where she employed fan dancers and served up drinks. And though she was arrested several times, she always avoided being charged by claiming she was just an employee and that customers brought in their own booze.

George Gershwin often played the piano at her joint, where she greeted her famous patrons with a hearty "Hello, suckers!" And those famous patrons—indeed, fans—were a virtual who's who of the day: Clara Bow, Gloria Swanson, Irving Berlin, John Barrymore, Peggy Hopkins Joyce, Reggie Vanderbilt, and Walter Chrysler.

When ever-enterprising "Texas" lost money during the Great Depression, she returned to film, playing—what else?—speakeasy owners in *Queen of the Nightclubs* (1929) and *Broadway Through a Keyhole* (1933). Though Texas died in the same year *Keyhole* was released—and just before Prohibition was repealed—she nonetheless managed to pass on her legacy: in 1932, Mae West launched her own career playing a version of Texas in the film *Night After Night*.

This drink, the Texas Twist, is as robust and spirited as its namesake.

TEXAS TWIST

5 fresh blueberries

¾ ounce ginger-infused simple syrup
(see recipe on page 205)

2 ounces North Shore Distiller's Gin No. 6

1 ounce fresh lime juice

Glass: Martini

Garnish: blueberries or a lime wheel

Chill a Martini glass. Add the blueberries and syrup to a cocktail shaker. Muddle them, then add the gin and lime juice. Add ice and shake well. Strain into the chilled glass. Garnish with a skewer of blueberries or a lime wheel.

The Rizzo

I do like a cocktail, a Pink Lady, before dinner.

—JAYNE MANSFIELD

Don't let the ponytails and poodle skirts fool you—the Pink Ladies of *Grease* were all about girl solidarity. And what feisty female doesn't love Rizzo, a girl who shimmies out a window with the parting zinger, "I'm gonna get my kicks while I'm still young enough to get 'em!" Sexually empowered and defiantly independent, she tells Sandy, "I can take care of myself . . . and anyone else who comes along."

Let's drink to Rizzo and her pink pals with this spin on the original **PINK LADY**.

THE RIZZO

¾ ounce gin

¾ ounce grenadine (see recipe on page 206)

3 ounces half-and-half

small cup of ice (about ½ cup)

Glass: coupe or Martini

Garnish: cherry

Add to a blender, one at a time, the gin, grenadine, half-and-half, and ice. Pulse the blender (on and off) until the mixture is nice and frothy. Pour into a glass and garnish with a cherry.

note

There is disagreement over whether this drink, also known as the **PINK SHIMMY**, is a proper Pink Lady. Some bartending enthusiasts believe that the correct recipe for the Pink Lady is as follows:

1½ ounces gin

½ ounce applejack whiskey

½ ounce fresh lemon juice

1 egg white

1 scant teaspoon grenadine

Add all the ingredients to a shaker without ice. Shake for 30 seconds. Then fill with ice and shake, vigorously, for about 2 minutes or until nice and frothy. Strain into a cocktail glass and garnish with a cherry.

Some other variations call for adding about ¾ ounce orange liqueur, like triple sec, into this mix and eliminating the egg white.

The Bechdel Test Drinking Game

———◦———

Named after author and cartoonist Alison Bechdel, the Bechdel Test measures just how feminist—or sexist—a movie, TV show, book, or other form of entertainment really is. This cultural measurement—sometimes known as the Bechdel-Wallace Test, as Bechdel credits her friend Liz Wallace for coming up with the idea—tests the sexism of fiction, usually film, by asking two questions: Does the work feature at least two women who talk to each other? And do the women talk to each other about something other than men? (Sometimes a third question is asked: Are the women identified by name?) If the answers to these questions are yes, the film passes the test. If the answers are no, the film fails.

Administer the test yourself by playing **THE BECHDEL TEST DRINKING GAME** while watching any movie, TV show, or video:

1. Take a sip when two women talk about a man for more than sixty seconds.

2. Take a sip when a man mentions a woman's appearance.

3. Take a sip when a woman disparages another woman's appearance.

4. Take a sip when two or more women talk about a man's job.

5. Take a sip when a woman over age twenty-one is called a "girl."

6. Take a sip when a woman is referred to as a babe, a bitch, a slut, or a whore.

7. Take a sip when two women shop together wearing high heels.

8. Take a sip when any high-heeled woman does something physically impossible in heels.

9. Take a sip when a woman is unnecessarily rescued by a man.

- *A League of Their Own*
- *Alien*
- *All About Eve*
- *Amélie*
- *Annie Hall*
- *Bonnie and Clyde*
- *Buffy the Vampire Slayer*
- *Erin Brockovich*
- *Funny Girl*
- *Network*
- *Nine to Five*
- *Pitch Perfect* and *Pitch Perfect 2*
- *Pulp Fiction*
- *Rear Window*
- *Romy and Michelle's High School Reunion*
- *Star Wars: The Force Awakens*
- *The DUFF*
- *The Help*
- *The Hunger Games*
- *Thelma & Louise*

In the mood to drink a lot? Try watching:

- Almost any other movie.

1950–2000

LIBATIONS

FOR THE

LIBERATED

Lucille's Balls

<hr>

Before Amy Schumer, Tina Fey, Amy Poehler, and Melissa McCarthy, there was LUCILLE BALL (1922–1989). She may have played a ditzy wife in *I Love Lucy*, but make no mistake— Lucille brilliantly paved the way for female comedians to rise to stardom.

Lucille launched the groundbreaking sitcom *I Love Lucy* when she was already forty years old—practically geriatric by Hollywood's standards. The show revolved around her both on- and offscreen—so much so that she insisted that her husband, Desi Arnaz, six years her junior, costar in her show, even though producers said he was "too ethnic." When she became pregnant with her second child in 1952, she didn't hide it, and thus became the first woman on television to be "expecting."

She was also a shrewd businesswoman. The company she shared with Desi, Desilu Productions, held the rights to her television series, which she and Desi produced using their own equipment. After Lucille divorced Desi in 1960, she bought him out of the studio; two years later, she became the first female CEO of a major television production company.

Carol Burnett told *People* magazine that, when Lucy took over her production company, she knew she had to be bold and take charge. "She said to me, 'Kid, that is when they put the *s* on the end of my last name.'"

Lucille eventually sold the company—it became Paramount Television—for a whopping $17 million.

What would be the perfect cocktail to honor this gutsy trailblazer? A 1950s mainstay, the **RUM AND COKE** or **CUBA LIBRE**.

LUCILLE'S BALLS

¼ ounce fresh lime juice

¼ ounce Fernet-Branca

1½ ounces Clément Select Barrel Rhum Agricole

2 to 3 ounces Mexican cane cola ("MexiCoke")

Glass: highball or Collins

Garnish: translucent straw

Pour the lime juice into a highball or Collins glass. Add the Fernet-Branca and Rhum Agricole. Add ice. Top off with the cola. Gently stir with a bar spoon and garnish with a straw.

Sylvia's Sword

I began to think vodka was my drink at last. It didn't taste like anything, but it went straight down into my stomach like a sword swallowers' sword and made me feel powerful and godlike.

— SYLVIA PLATH, from *The Bell Jar*

Haunted and prolific, SYLVIA PLATH (1932–1963) recounted in *The Bell Jar* her own story of the implosion of the perfect life. Ahead of her time, Sylvia wrote of a woman's yearning to discover herself and to be herself—which put her at odds with mid-century society's limiting roles for women.

Though it's true that Sylvia was known to drink vodka straight from a jar or bottle, a cocktail honoring her deserves a little punch. So here's a sweet, dark-colored **WINTER PUNCH**, which can be imbibed warm or cold, as the seasons or your moods dictate.

SYLVIA'S SWORD

6 ounces vodka

4 ounces crème de violette

8 ounces freshly brewed and cooled Earl Grey tea, or tea syrup (see recipe on page 214)

4 ounces pomegranate or cranberry juice

2 ounces oleo saccharum (see note, below)

1 ounce grenadine

4 dashes orange bitters

3 cups sparkling water (if serving cold)

Glass: a bell jar, of course

Garnish: 1 lemon or orange, thinly sliced

Pour vodka, crème de violette, Earl Grey tea, pomegranate or cranberry juice, oleo saccharum, grenadine, and orange bitters into a quart-sized mason jar and shake. For warm punch, simply pour the mixture into individual teacups and serve.

(continued on next page)

SYLVIA'S SWORD

For cold punch, pour the mixture into a small punch bowl and top with up to an equal amount of sparkling water, to taste. Add ice: at least ¾ cup per serving, or about 3 to 4 cups. (This recipe makes about 4 to 6 drinks of cold punch, depending on how much sparkling water is added.)

note

Oft considered the secret ingredient in punches, oleo saccharum is basically a combination of citrus oil and sugar. Bartender Lauren Myerscough and her husband Max Messier sell their excellent handmade Cocktail & Sons oleo saccharum at www.cocktailandsons.com. You can also make your own; see the recipe on page 212.

Ruth's Pink Taboo

Before Disney's princesses came into power, before American Girls went on any of their wholesome, life-enhancing adventures, and before Bratzes' big heads sassed the playground, there was Barbie, and little girls loved her.

Classic Punch Formula

1 part "sour" (citrus)

2 parts "sweet" (sugar)

3 parts "strong" (booze)

4 parts "weak" (spices or tea)

While scholars have argued against everything Barbie—from her unrealistic proportions to her pinkalicious lifestyle—what many may not realize is that this cultural icon was created by a feminist entrepreneur and mother.

At a time when baby dolls were all the rage, RUTH HANDLER (1916–2002) recognized a common truth that male toy company executives just couldn't see. Little girls didn't always want to play moms to baby dolls; they also wanted to pretend to be teenagers who wore makeup and got ready for dates—and who were arguably much more fun and exciting than were moms. In fact, Ruth got the idea for Barbie by watching her own daughter, Barbara, play with paper dolls that were drawn to look like teenagers. When Ruth first presented the idea to execs, they were aghast at the thought of producing a doll with breasts, saying no mother would buy her daughter such a big-bosomed toy. But sure of herself and her market, Ruth persevered—and in Barbie's first year, more than 350,000 dolls were sold, establishing the pert plastic fashion model firmly in the toy aisles of stores everywhere.

In later years, Ruth—and Barbie—both evolved. Barbie became a doctor, explored space, and drove a NASCAR race car, while Ruth quietly survived breast cancer and then, not so quietly, trailblazed a second career as a breast-prosthesis manufacturer. She even became a spokeswoman for self-exams and early detection at a time when the subject remained taboo. "I've lived my life from breast to breast," Ruth quipped.

Just as the idea of Barbie was subversive, so is this pink drink. A pink cocktail doesn't have to cloy with sweetness or hit you over the head with fruitiness. Instead, much like Ruth, this is both complex and delicious. And it's best enjoyed in a sparkly crystal glass.

RUTH'S PINK TABOO

1 ounce Bols genever

1 ounce Jim Beam rye

¾ ounce grenadine

¼ ounce lemon juice

1 dash of Bar Keep Baked Apple bitters

1 egg white

Glass: coupe

Garnish: Peychaud's bitters

Place genever, rye, grenadine, lemon juice, Bar Keep Baked Apple bitters, and egg white into a cocktail shaker, without ice, and shake vigorously for 1 minute. (This, in bar parlance, is called the "dry shake.") Add ice, and shake vigorously for 1 to 2 minutes more. Strain into a coupe glass, and add 1 dash Peychaud's bitters on top.

The Family That Drinks Together . . .

With businesses in the 1960s desperate to capture the emerging "family market"—think *Mad Men* and their Burger Chef accounts—restaurants started creating separate bar spaces attached to the main dining rooms, so the family could enjoy a dinner, and then Dad and maybe even Mom could slip over to the bar next door for a nightcap. Some appropriately called them "family-style" bars, where, fortuitously, women who worked as waitresses, hostesses, and cooks at the restaurants could be promoted to bartender. Because, of course, it was less objectionable for a woman to mix a Martini at a family restaurant's bar than for her to pour a shot of bourbon at a corner tavern.

From this period forward, changes in drinking practices benefitted women. By the mid-sixties, nearly two-thirds of all alcohol was consumed at home or in private clubs. So, needing to reassert their relevancy, bars evolved into pubs or gathering spaces for darts, pool, and anything else to lure butts onto barstools. And when bars are hungry for business, they are more welcoming to women. Better yet, some bars targeted couples—thus giving rise to the cocktail lounge.

Bra Burner

MARCY SKOWRONSKI has inspired legions of bartenders in Milwaukee, Wisconsin. In 2016, at the age of ninety, Marcy still tends bar at her beloved Holler House, which *Esquire* magazine called one of the "best bars in America." (It also happens to be where you'll find the oldest bowling lanes in the country.) Marcy serves up plenty of bawdy fun with her drinks. In the 1960s, Marcy and her partaking pals started a tradition of removing their bras and hanging them from the fixtures—after autographing them, of course. Soon, hundreds of bras of all colors and sizes dangled from the ceiling.

The bras remained on display for close to fifty years—until a city inspector declared them a fire hazard and insisted they be taken down. In this case, bra burning didn't seem to be a likely risk, so Marcy protested the takedown—and won. The bar held a celebration and returned the lacy decor to their rightful spots. To this day, women still contribute their bras, autographing them before throwing them to the ceiling.

Marcy's spirit of choice has always been vodka, usually flavored with lime. She loves limes so much that, back when bars didn't use fresh fruits, she used to carry them in her purse when she barhopped. So an ideal cocktail for Marcy is the GIMLET, made from lime, simple syrup, and vodka. Milwaukee bartender Katie Rose dresses up this Gimlet by using a ginger-honey syrup instead of simple syrup. She also uses Rehorst vodka infused with Rishi mint green tea. Why? Because both Rishi and Rehorst are products of Milwaukee, just like Marcy.

BRA BURNER

2 ounces Rishi mint green tea–infused Rehorst vodka (see note, below)

½ ounce fresh lime juice

½ ounce ginger honey syrup or tea syrup (see recipes on pages 205 and 214)

Glass: Martini or coupe

Garnish: lime twist and fresh mint leaves

Fill a shaker with ice. Add the vodka, lime juice, and syrup. Shake for at least 30 seconds or until chilled. Strain into a Martini or coupe glass; garnish with a lime twist and fresh mint leaves.

note

To infuse vodka with Rishi mint green tea, place 2 tablespoons Rishi mint green tea into 750 milliliters vodka (one standard bottle). Shake and let sit for 10 to 15 minutes, then strain.

Sister Solidaritea

On August 26, 1970, more than five thousand women hung up their aprons, put away their pot holders, and linked arms to march down Fifth Avenue in Manhattan. Their goal: to draw attention to the unequal distribution of domestic labor by staging a workers' "strike." Carrying signs with slogans like "Don't Iron While the Strike Is Hot," the marchers sparked enough enthusiasm to inspire similar events in ninety cities and forty-two states.

That's solidarity.

A properly made **LONG ISLAND ICED TEA** calls for equal amounts of vodka, gin, rum, tequila, and orange liqueur, topped with cola and a splash of sweet and sour. The traditional recipe uses triple sec, but a higher-quality liqueur like Cointreau or Grand Marnier definitely ups the taste factor. Also, use a really high-quality cola like Q Kola. And while some recipes call for just ¾ to 1 ounce of cola, others call for up to 3 ounces. We think the sweet spot is 2¼ ounces cola, but you should start with ¾ ounce and keep adding to your taste.

SISTER SOLIDARITEA

½ ounce vodka

½ ounce gin

½ ounce rum

½ ounce tequila

½ ounce orange liqueur

¼ ounce simple syrup (see recipe on page 201)

¼ ounce fresh lemon juice, plus ½ teaspoon
(1 lemon wedge)

2¼ ounces cola

Glass: Collins or pint

Garnish: lemon wedge

Fill a Collins or pint glass with ice. Add the vodka,
gin, rum, tequila, orange liqueur, simple syrup,
and lemon juice. Stir briskly to chill. Pour into
a shaker, add the cola, give one or two quick
shakes, then pour back into the glass. Stir in the
remaining ½ teaspoon lemon juice and garnish
with a lemon wedge.

Bloody Mary
✦ Richards ✦

Almost fifty years after Mary Tyler Moore's character MARY RICHARDS first tossed her blue beret into the air on the streets of Minneapolis, people are still talking about her groundbreaking role on *The Mary Tyler Moore Show*. As a never-married, independent career woman, Mary was a novelty. She sought personal and professional fulfillment, and she inspired countless women to pursue their dreams—some to great heights. Oprah noted that "Mary Tyler Moore has had more influence on my career than any other single person."

Of course, Mary Richards's namesake drink has to be the **BLOODY MARY**.

BLOODY MARY RICHARDS

8 ounces tomato juice

1 ounce beef stock

1 teaspoon Worcestershire sauce

1 teaspoon olive brine

1 teaspoon pickle juice

⅛ teaspoon freshly cracked black pepper
(about 5 full rotations of a pepper mill at the
medium setting)

⅛ teaspoon or 1 dash celery salt

⅛ teaspoon freshly prepared horseradish,
or to taste

⅛ teaspoon Sambal oelek or another hot sauce,
or to taste

⅛ teaspoon Crystal hot sauce or another hot
sauce, or to taste

2 to 3 ounces vodka

3 ounces beer

Glass: pint, plus tiny pint for beer

Garnish: see garnish note, next page

(continued on next page)

BLOODY MARY RICHARDS

a note on preparation

If you like, you can make the tomato base in advance; in fact, some recommend letting the flavors marinate for at least one day. You can store the mixture in the refrigerator for up to a week. If you plan to make enough for several drinks, be sure to multiply the recipe quantities for the total number of servings desired.

To make the tomato base, add the tomato juice, beef stock, Worcestershire sauce, olive brine, pickle juice, black pepper, celery salt, horseradish, Sambal oelek (if using), and Crystal hot sauce (if using) to a large shaker without ice. Shake until well combined.

To make the cocktail, fill a pint glass with ice. Fill a shaker with ice. Add the tomato base mixture (about 9½ ounces per drink if you made a batch) and vodka. Shake hard for 30 to 60 seconds. Strain into the prepared pint glass.

a note on the garnish

Try Roth jalapeño Havarti and Roth chipotle Havarti cheese. You can also set up a garnish bar with celery, lime, lemon, romaine fronds, shrimp, beef jerky, Swiss chard fronds, pickled okra, pickled cauliflower, olives, hearts of palm, pickles, prime rib cubes, fried chicken, oysters, scallops . . . The combinations are as endless as your imagination.

variations

Just as with the garnishes, there are many variations to choose from. Some add a bit of flair to their Bloody Marys by rimming the glasses with celery salt. To do this, sprinkle celery salt on a small plate. Wipe a wedge of lime around the rim of the glass, then twirl the rim in the celery salt. Others add ⅛ teaspoon smoky Spanish paprika to the cocktail itself. Some add ¼ to ½ ounce lemon or lime juice to the cocktail. Others still add a dash of simple syrup or sugar.

Many mixologists play with the basic seasonings in the tomato base to create their own personal flavor profile. To make this cocktail more upscale, make fresh tomato juice, especially when tomatoes are in season. To make this a Bloody Maria, use tequila instead of vodka.

Kissed by a Wookie

In a memorable scene of *The Empire Strikes Back*, Princess Leia follows Han Solo down a frozen corridor on the ice planet Hoth. When Han proffers, "Afraid I was going to leave without giving you a good-bye kiss?" Leia replies, "I'd just as soon kiss a wookie!"

For all the valid complaints about the dearth of female characters in the original *Star Wars* universe, let's not forget that Princess Leia was anything but a doormat. She might have initially needed rescuing, but in the midst of Han and Luke's dithering, she took charge, shooting a hole into the trash compactor to provide a memorable—and aromatic—escape. She wielded a blaster like no man's business, never gave up on the Rebel Alliance, and never compromised her principles. She saved Luke when his hand was cut off by Darth Vader, strangled Jabba the Hutt in a bikini, and shot down Stormtroopers so that Han and Chewie could shut down the force field of the new Death Star. In the new trilogy, she's a general. What's not to love?

Like Princess Leia, Kissed by a Wookie is both strong and feminine. This cocktail serves up a balanced mix of Kahlúa, rum, and Tuaca (which, in case you didn't notice, rhymes with our favorite wookie's name). For fun, serve with a pair of matched cinnamon buns topped with chocolate ganache.

KISSED BY A WOOKIE

½ ounce Tuaca

½ ounce Kahlúa

½ ounce white or dark rum

3 small scoops chocolate ice cream

Glass: Martini or poco grande

Garnish: whipped cream, cherry, and shaved chocolate

Place all the ingredients in a blender. Blend for 2 to 3 minutes or until creamy and smooth. Pour into a Martini or poco grande glass. Top with a dollop of whipped cream, a cherry, and a sprinkling of shaved chocolate.

Get Up and Go-Go

THE GO-GO'S rode the new wave of history with their punk-power sound, becoming the first—and still only—all-female band to write their own songs, play their own instruments, and steer their own sound all the way to the top of the charts.

What kind of cocktail should honor the rocking trail they've blazed? Something coconutty and exotic, transporting us away on . . . vacation.

Here's a spin on the **BUSHWACKER**, a delectable drink created by Linda Murphy, former owner of the Sandshaker Beach Bar on Florida's Pensacola Beach. Creamy, Kahlúa-y, and coconutty, with a splash of strong rum on top, this drink became popular throughout its panhandle city. In fact, it became so popular that in 1986 the city launched an annual Bushwacker Festival, which to this day features live bands, festive foods, and a 5K race.

GET UP AND GO-GO

1½ ounces Kahlúa or other coffee liqueur

1½ ounces white crème de cacao

1½ ounces whole milk

¾ ounce Coco López or other coconut cream

1 heaping cup ice

¾ ounce Bacardi 151 rum, Sailor Jerry Spiced 92-proof rum, or regular white rum

Glass: hurricane or poco grande

Garnish: cherry

Pour the Kahlúa or coffee liqueur, white crème de cacao, milk, Coco López or coconut cream, and ice into a blender. Blend until creamy and frothy. Pour into a hurricane or poco grande glass. Next, "float" the rum on top: slowly pour the rum over an inverted teaspoon (with the round side up). Garnish with a cherry.

variations

Instead of rum, you could add a float of flavored vodka, like Stoli Salted Karamel. To create a banana wacker, add ¼ banana to the blender. To make a banana split wacker, add ¾ ounce Godiva chocolate liqueur and a cherry to the blender. To make a strawberry wacker, add 4 small strawberries to the blender.

Gloria Stein'Em

She went undercover to investigate sexism in the Playboy Club. She spoke out against discrimination, and defended rights for women and people of color. She founded a kick-ass magazine. She wrote one of the funniest essays *ever*, "If Men Could Menstruate." (It's available online—read it and weep with laughter!) She famously said, "A gender-equal society would be one where the word 'gender' does not exist: where everyone can be themselves."

We're glad you're you, GLORIA STEINEM! We toast you by raising our beer stein'ems filled with this recipe for the **SHANDY**.

GLORIA STEIN'EM

8 ounces favorite brew

2 cups lemonade

Glass: two steins or pint glasses

Garnish: lemon wedges

Fill two steins or pint glasses with ice. Divide the beer between the two. Divide the lemonade between the two. Garnish each with a lemon wedge.

note

A proper shandy is made with equal parts beer and lemonade and/or soda. As you might imagine, the better the beer, the better the shandy—and the better the lemonade, the better the shandy. Homemade lemonade is best, but some stores sell freshly made lemonade.

The Mint Juleps

In 1987, an all-women band in London, THE MINT JULEPS, recorded a song called "Girl to the Power of Six." A lyric in that song launched the term "girl power"—now an everyday reference to female empowerment and independence. Here's a playlist of more feminist anthems to blast while stirring up a MINT JULEP of your own:

ALICIA KEYS . . . . "GIRL ON FIRE"

ANI DIFRANCO . . . . "NOT A PRETTY GIRL"

ARETHA FRANKLIN . . . ."RESPECT"

BEYONCÉ . . . . "RUN THE WORLD"

BIKINI KILL . . . . "REBEL GIRL"

BRITNEY SPEARS . . . ."STRONGER"

CHAKA KHAN . . . . "I'M EVERY WOMAN"

CHRISTINA AGUILERA. . . . "CAN'T HOLD US DOWN"

DAR WILLIAMS . . . . "WHEN I WAS A BOY"

DESTINY'S CHILD . . . . . . "INDEPENDENT WOMEN"

DIXIE CHICKS . . . . "GOODBYE EARL"

DOLLY PARTON . . . . "JUST BECAUSE I'M A WOMAN"

HELEN REDDY. . . . . "I AM WOMAN"

JANELLE MONÁE AND ERYKAH BADU. . . "Q.U.E.E.N."

JANET JACKSON . . . . "CONTROL"

JEANNIE C. RILEY. . . . . . ."HARPER VALLEY P.T.A."

JOAN JETT . . . . "BAD REPUTATION"

KELLY CLARKSON. . . . . . . "MISS INDEPENDENT"

LE TIGRE . . . ."HOT TOPIC"

MADONNA . . . ."EXPRESS YOURSELF"

MARTINA MCBRIDE . . . ."INDEPENDENCE DAY"

MARY CHAPIN CARPENTER . . ."I TAKE MY CHANCES"

MEREDITH BROOKS. . . . . "BITCH"

NO DOUBT . . . . "JUST A GIRL"

P!NK . . . ."MOST GIRLS"

QUEEN LATIFAH. . . . . "U.N.I.T.Y."

SINÉAD O'CONNOR . . . . "RED FOOTBALL"

SLEATER-KINNEY . . . ."#1 MUST HAVE"

SPICE GIRLS . . . . "WANNABE"

THE PUSSYCAT DOLLS . . . ."WHATCHA THINK
ABOUT THAT"

THE MINT JULEPS

2 ounces bourbon

1½ ounces mint sugar syrup (see note, below)

½ ounce water

4 mint leaves

Glass: julep cup, Collins, or rocks

Garnish: mint sprig

Fill a julep cup or Collins or rocks glass with ice. Fill a shaker with ice. Add the bourbon, mint sugar syrup, water, and mint leaves to the shaker, and shake, hard, for about 10 seconds. Pour the mixture into the prepared cup or glass and garnish with a sprig of mint.

note

A proper julep is made with spearmint, not peppermint. But if you want to make the best juleps, get some Kentucky Colonel mint, which was cultivated just for the julep.

Buffy's Stake

Until Buffy came along in 1992, most women in horror films either suffered terrible deaths or were rescued by burly men. Not Buffy Anne Summers. Joss Whedon's heroine could stake a vampire as easily as she could cheer her high school's football team. She remains the ultimate feminist vampire-staker, and her story reinvented the horror genre.

Since Buffy appropriately staked, shot, and stoned any number of horrific bad guys, a drink to honor her has to have a stake—er, stone—in it, and in this case, it's the **STONE SOUR**. A stone sour is made with either liquor or liqueur, usually with a ratio of 1½ ounces booze to 2 ounces juice to 1 ounce sour mix. Instead of a premixed sour, this recipe calls for simple syrup and lemon juice. A classic stone sour is often made with amaretto or whiskey, but you can also try Tuaca, Frangelico, or an orange liqueur like Cointreau. And you can't go wrong with bourbon, vodka, or gin, either.

For a delicious variation, use blood orange juice and/or Meyer lemon juice.

BUFFY'S STAKE

1½ ounces liquor or liqueur

2 ounces fresh orange juice

½ ounce fresh lemon juice

½ ounce simple syrup (see recipe on page 201)

Glass: rocks or Collins

Garnish: half-moon orange slice and (maraschino) cherry "flag"

Fill a rocks or Collins glass with ice. Fill a shaker with ice. Add all the ingredients to the shaker and shake for 30 to 60 seconds. Strain into the prepared glass. Garnish with a "flag": wrap the half-moon orange slice around a cherry or maraschino cherry, then secure it with a toothpick or cocktail umbrella.

2000s

STIRRING UP

COCKTAILS

SHAKING
UP *the*
World

Anarchy Amaretto

What if we lived in a world where women didn't have to be concerned about their looks? What if we lived in a world where women didn't worry about walking alone at night? What if equality wasn't a concept yet to be grasped but a reality in which we all already lived?

Some might say this is anarchy. Others would call it a fantasy. Too bad we don't have a fairy godmother to wave her magic wand and make it come true. Since we don't, allow us to present to you Anarchy Amaretto, a variation of the classic GODMOTHER drink.

The base of the Godmother is vodka, with just enough amaretto to liven things up. We also add a dash of bitters and maraschino liqueur for good measure.

ANARCHY AMARETTO

1½ ounces vodka

½ ounce amaretto

¼ ounce maraschino liqueur

dash Angostura bitters or other bitters

Glass: rocks if on the rocks; coupe or Martini if straight up

Garnish: cherry

If serving on the rocks, fill a rocks glass with ice. Fill a large glass with ice. Add vodka, amaretto, maraschino liqueur, and bitters and stir. Strain into the rocks glass, or a coupe or Martini glass if serving straight up. Garnish with a cherry.

BFF

Thelma and Louise. Rachel and Monica. Oprah and Gayle. Tina and Amy. There's nothing like knowing your bestie has your back.

Expert mixologist Debbi Peek was inspired to create this cocktail for her own best friend, Lynn House; she calls it "A Peek in Your House." You can call it whatever you like—as long as you enjoy it while toasting a wingwoman in your life.

BFF

1½ ounces VSOP Cognac

1 ounce ginger liqueur

1 ounce fresh lemon juice

1 ounce honey-rosemary syrup
(see recipe on page 208)

Glass: Martini or coupe

Garnish: lemon wheel and rosemary sprig

Chill a Martini or coupe glass. Fill a shaker with
ice. Add all the ingredients and shake. Strain into
the chilled glass. Garnish with a lemon wheel
and rosemary sprig.

Girl Power Sour

"Sugar and spice and everything nice, that's what little girls are made of." And so goes the oft-quoted nursery rhyme. No surprise, it was made popular by a *man*. We always thought snails and puppy dog tails were more interesting.

Instead of sugar and spice, go sour—**WHISKEY SOUR**, that is. While you can make this cocktail with simple syrup, this recipe shows another technique, with fast-dissolving superfine sugar.

GIRL POWER SOUR

1½ ounces whiskey

2 ounces fresh lemon juice

1 egg white

1½ teaspoons extra-fine sugar

Glass: rocks or Collins

Garnish: half-moon orange slice and (maraschino) cherry "flag"

Fill a rocks or Collins glass with ice. Fill a shaker with ice. Add all the ingredients and shake hard for 1 to 2 minutes. Strain into the prepared glass. To make the orange "flag" garnish, wrap a half-moon orange slice around a cherry or maraschino cherry, then secure it with a toothpick or cocktail umbrella.

note

You can vary both the booze and the juice to create different varieties of sours.

The F Word

Feminist.

Feminist, feminist, feminist, feminist, feminist.

There, we said it. Whether you're climbing the corporate ladder, staying home with your kiddos, balancing work and family, or still figuring out your place in the world, if you believe women are equal to men, you're a feminist.

Since it takes mojo to work toward equality in an unequal world, let's drink a MOJITO, and say it all together, one more time...

Feminist.

THE F WORD

1 mint sprig

2 lime wedges

10 to 15 mint leaves

1½ ounces rum

¾ ounce fresh lime juice

¾ ounce simple syrup (see recipe on page 201)

3 ounces seltzer water or club soda

dash citrus bitters

Glass: Collins

Garnish: additional mint sprig plus lime wheel or wedge

Fill a Collins glass with ice. With a muddler or muddling substitute, gently press the mint sprig into the bottom of a Collins glass, swirling. Press the leaves around the rim, then discard the sprig. Add the mint leaves and lime wedges to the shaker. Muddle gently to express their oils and juice. Add rum, lime juice, simple syrup, and ice.

(continued on next page)

THE F WORD

Shake for 1 minute, then strain into the glass. Top with seltzer or club soda, and garnish with an additional mint sprig and lime wheel or wedge. To finish, add a dash of citrus bitters on top.

note

This is a refreshing and not-too-sweet Mojito. If you find this one not sweet enough, add more simple syrup in ¼-ounce increments until you achieve your perfect sweetness.

also

If you aren't adept at muddling, you can replace the simple syrup with mint simple syrup (see recipe on page 210). But note that, to get the proper mint flavor, you'll need to use 1 ounce mint syrup instead of the ¾ ounce for just simple syrup. Since that makes the drink a touch sweeter, you might want to add a bit more citrus bitters to help balance out the flavor.

Mind the (Wage) Gap

Yes, we mind the gap. Very much, thank you. The wage gap, that is. All we want is equal pay for equal work, $1 to a woman for every $1 to a man. Not too much to ask, is it?

Since women are, still, screwed—earning only 77 cents per every dollar men earn—the appropriate drink for women suffering from Pay Prejudice is the **SCREWDRIVER**.

The basic Screwdriver is just vodka and (canned or bottled) orange juice. To make the best Screw-it-to-'em-driver ever, use freshly squeezed oranges. Either use your favorite vodka or, for a variation, use a citrus-based vodka like Sol for some extra oomph. Then add a dash or dropper of your favorite orange bitters. But we're not bitter. Really.

MIND THE [WAGE] GAP

1½ ounces vodka

3 ounces fresh orange juice

dash or dropper orange bitters

Glass: Collins or rocks

Garnish: orange wedge

Fill a Collins or rocks glass with ice. Fill a shaker with ice. Add all the ingredients and shake for 30 seconds or until chilled. Strain into the prepared glass and garnish with an orange wedge.

variations

The Screwdriver is just one of a plethora of vodka-and-juice drinks. Change up the juices, and you've got different drinks. Replace with grapefruit juice, and you've got a Greyhound. Use cranberry, and you've got a Cape Cod. Rim the glass with salt, and you've got a Salty Dog. And if you use 2 ounces orange juice and 1 ounce cranberry, you've got yourself a Sea Breeze.

Little Black Dress

The **MARTINI** is the little black dress of cocktails. It never goes out of style, and one of its best features is its ease in being perfectly accessorized for any occasion.

Dress it up with olives, citrus twists, and pickled pearl onions. Add a splash of olive juice. And just as a black dress can be made of silk or linen, the LBD drink can be made with either gin or vodka.

Choose a gin or a vodka you really enjoy; while sours, Collinses, and juice-based drinks can hide the taste of a bad gin or an inferior vodka, all the good or bad flavors of the base spirit shine through in a Martini. However, a good spirit doesn't have to be the most expensive bottle in the liquor store; it just has to be one you like.

In the making of a Martini, after pouring the gin or vodka, you add a touch of dry vermouth. And here's where Martini-making gets tricky. Originally, the recipe called for equal amounts of gin and vermouth, but as the drink evolved, the ratio became three or four parts gin to one part vermouth. Some dry Martini drinkers want just a teensy tiny splash of vermouth.

LITTLE BLACK DRESS

4 ounces gin or vodka

¼ to 1 ounce vermouth

Glass: Martini or coupe

Garnish: olive, lemon twist, and/or pearl onions

Chill a coupe or Martini glass until nearly frosty. (You might fill it with water and ice to get it extra frosty.) Add ice to the bottom part of a shaker or large glass. Add the gin or vodka, then the vermouth. Stir until chilled—about 10 to 15 brisk but not violent stirs. Empty the chilled glass of its ice and water. Strain the drink into the glass and garnish.

a few words about garnishing the martini

Traditionally, a Martini is garnished with a single glorious pimento-stuffed olive. But you can fancy it up with a blue cheese-stuffed olive, an artisanally brined olive, or any other olive of your choosing.

- You can also garnish your drink with a citrus twist. If you do, be sure to twist the garnish over the drink before you drop it in, so that the oils land on the surface, adding an aromatic burst.

- Note that if you garnish a Martini with three small pickled pearl onions and a lemon twist, it's no longer a Martini—it's a Gibson.

variations

For a very dry Martini, instead of adding the vermouth to the mixing glass, drizzle it right into the serving glass, then swirl it and pour out the excess before adding the chilled gin or vodka.

For a dirty Martini, add about ¼ to ½ ounce olive juice before stirring or shaking. Note that many bartenders recommend shaking this type of Martini.

Crème de la Femme

Of all the creamy after-dinner dessert drinks, perhaps none is more famous than the **GRASSHOPPER**. This drink first started appearing in bars sometime in the middle of the twentieth century, and once it made its way into supper clubs and classic cocktail lounges, it never left.

Imagine yourself swooning to Sinatra while sipping this sweet indulgence, surrounded by white jackets, black bowties, strapless pink dresses, and pin curls . . .

Then shake off the vision, return to the modern world, and be glad you can still enjoy the green goddess of cocktails without all that fancy fuss.

CRÈME DE LA FEMME

¾ ounce green crème de menthe

¾ ounce white crème de cacao

3 ounces half-and-half

½ cup ice

Glass: Martini, coupe, or poco grande

Garnish (optional): whipped cream, Andes mint, mint sprig, chocolate shavings mixed with sugar, cocoa powder, or chocolate syrup

Pour the green crème de menthe and white crème de cacao into a blender. Top with the ice and half-and-half. Turn the blender on for 5 seconds, then turn it off; repeat 3 or 4 times or until the cream is foamy.

(continued on next page)

CRÈME DE LA FEMME

a note about the garnish

Traditionally, the Grasshopper does not have a garnish, but this is where you can get creative.

- You could drizzle chocolate syrup in the glass before you pour in the cocktail.

- You could dust the top of the drink with cocoa powder.

- Or how about rimming the glass with finely shaved chocolate mixed with sugar?

- Perhaps add a dollop of whipped cream— on which you could place a single Andes mint, or even a fresh sprig of mint.

note

This recipe converts easily into an ice cream version: just substitute the half-and-half and ice with one large scoop (about ¾ cup) vanilla ice cream.

Cocktail Crusader

Women now make up 60 percent of all American bartenders, and they're also distilling whiskey, promoting spirits as brand ambassadors, and rising through the ranks as executives.

It's all thanks to trailblazers like Julie Reiner, author of *The Craft Cocktail Party* and visionary behind such top-tier bars as The Flatiron Lounge and the Pegu Club. Not that it came easily for her. Early in her career in New York City, she had a hard time finding regular work as a bartender.

"I would walk in to apply for a job, and they'd say, 'Are you sure you don't want to cocktail waitress?'" she recalls. "It was all men behind the bar."

Reiner eventually proved her skills and gained acclaim as bar owner, beverage director, and master mixologist. Her recipes have been featured in *The New York Times*, *New York Magazine*, *Food & Wine*, *Imbibe*, *The Wall Street Journal*, *Esquire*, and more.

"Julie helped pioneer this movement," says Katie Stipe, mixologist for Diageo Global Spirits Company and beverage manager for The Vine. "Julie has always been a great mentor, and she's a badass bartender. Now, it's no longer a boy's club."

Consensual Sex on the Beach

◆———◆

No means no. Yes means yes. It's that simple.

A bartender in Fort Lauderdale in the 1980s created the original SEX ON THE BEACH cocktail using a blend of vodka, peach schnapps, orange juice, and cranberry juice. Pretty soon spring-breakers and beach-partiers had to have this drink just so they could say, "I went to Florida and had sex on the beach."

Variations of the drink soon followed, swapping the schnapps for Midori liqueur and sometimes adding a touch of raspberry Chambord liqueur. Others like to replace the orange juice with pineapple juice.

To update this recipe a bit, we switched out the schnapps for a peach liqueur, and we replaced cranberry juice with raspberry juice.

CONSENSUAL SEX ON THE BEACH

1½ ounces regular vodka or citrus vodka

½ ounce peach liqueur, such as Mathilde

¼ ounce Chambord or other raspberry liqueur (optional)

2 ounces fresh raspberry juice or raspberry all-juice blend

2 ounces fresh orange juice

dash orange bitters

Glass: highball

Garnish: orange wheel and cherry, of course!

Fill a highball glass with ice. Fill a shaker with ice. Add all the ingredients and shake for 1 minute. Strain into the prepared glass and garnish with a orange wheel and a cherry.

Perfect Cut

Forget diamonds. This cocktail is your new best friend.

PERFECT CUT

1½ ounces Absolut Elyx vodka

1 ounce Lillet Rosé (a French aperitif wine)

4 dashes Regan's Orange Bitters No. 6

Glass: rocks

Prepare a rocks glass with one large piece of ice, preferably one that is diamond-shaped. Fill a shaker or glass with ice. Add all the ingredients and stir. Strain into the prepared rocks glass.

I went out with a guy who once told me I didn't need to drink to make myself more fun to be around. I told him, "I'm drinking so that you're more fun to be around."

—CHELSEA HANDLER

Are You There, Vodka? It's Me, Chelsea

Mud Mask

You won't need a day at the spa to enjoy this spin on the classic MUDSLIDE.

MUD MASK

1 ounce Baileys Irish Cream or other Irish cream liqueur

1 ounce vodka

1 ounce Kahlúa or other coffee liqueur

½ to ¾ cup ice

½ ounce half-and-half (optional)

Glass: Martini, coupe, or poco grande

Garnish: whipped cream, chocolate shavings, and/or chocolate syrup

Add all the ingredients to a blender. Blend until smooth. Pour into a Martini, coupe, or poco grande glass. Garnish with whipped cream, chocolate shavings, and/or chocolate syrup.

Cocktails for a Cause: Speed Rack Competition

Think you can mix it up with the best? Enter the Speed Rack competition, where top female bartenders compete in a series of timed and judged challenges.

Ivy Mix and Lynette Marrero founded Speed Rack in 2011 to combat sexism in the industry.

"You either weren't hired because you were a woman or you were hired because you were a woman," Mix says. Ivy approached Marrero, who was president of the New York chapter of Ladies United for the Preservation of the Endangered Cocktail, and the two of them decided to try out one competition—they gathered a group of talented women to compete, and used the competition as an opportunity to raise money for charity. That first event was a success, so they took their idea national. Since then, hundreds of top female bartenders have competed, and more than $350,000 has been raised for breast-cancer charities.

Caitlin Laman, the bar manager at Trick Dog in San Francisco who won Speed Rack USA in 2014, explains how the competition works: "They give you a list of sixty drinks, and you get on stage and make four drinks as fast and as well as you can," she says. "It's really fun, and really stressful. I feel very, very fortunate to have won."

Grown-up Girl Scout

Girl Scouting isn't all about campouts and lanyards—it also promotes financial and intellectual independence and an empowered, adventurous spirit. Its national governing board has boasted progressive members such as feminist icon Betty Friedan, and the Girl Scout Advocacy Network prides itself on annual lobbying in Washington, DC on behalf of girls.

You may be too old to join a Girl Scout troop, but you can still earn a merit badge. Follow the recipe below, and wear your emblem with pride.

GROWN-UP GIRL SCOUT

¾ ounce Rumple Minze peppermint schnapps

¾ ounce Godiva Dark Chocolate Liqueur

½ ounce Bushwacker mix, or add to taste
(see "Get Up and Go-Go" Bushwacker recipe
on page 138)

Glass: shot

Fill a shaker with ice. Add all the ingredients and
shake for at least 1 minute or until well combined.
Pour into a large shot glass.

Mother's Little Helper

This cocktail is as warm as an embrace, which every mother needs after a long day of catering to tiny people with sticky fingers and irrational demands for more Cheerios.

This is also a perfect drink for a fall evening, or to accompany a Thanksgiving dinner, or to toast our mothers, and their mothers, and theirs.

MOTHER'S LITTLE HELPER

1½ ounces brandy

½ ounce Tuaca

3 ounces honey crisp apple cider

Glass: rocks if serving on the rocks; coupe if serving straight up

Garnish: apple sliver

If serving on the rocks, fill a rocks glass with ice. Fill a shaker with ice. Add all the ingredients and shake for 30 seconds. Strain into either the prepared rocks glass or, if serving straight up, into an elegant coupe glass. Garnish with a single apple sliver.

Multitasking Womanhattan

◆───────◆───────◆

Named for the glorious metropolis of New York City, the **MANHATTAN** conjures images of backroom deals, cigar smoke, and a raw sort of power.

Today's woman has power, too. The power to do it all—from the babies to the boardrooms. After a long day of juggling, give yourself a well-earned rest with this cocktail at your side.

Traditionally the Manhattan is made with 1½ ounces whiskey or bourbon and ½ ounce sweet vermouth, with the traditional garnish of a sweet maraschino cherry. Variations include the dry Manhattan, made with dry vermouth and garnished with an olive; a perfect Manhattan, made with equal parts dry and sweet vermouths and garnished with a lemon twist; and a Southern Comfort Manhattan, made with 1½ ounces So Co and ½ ounce dry vermouth with a garnish of two cherries.

Now, a good standard Manhattan calls for bitters, and usually it's Angostura bitters, but other bitters (such as orange) can also be used. Just a dash or a dropper brings out the spicy and sweet notes of both the whiskey and the vermouth.

MULTITASKING WOMANHATTAN

1½ ounces Bulleit Bourbon

¾ ounce Carpano Antica Formula sweet vermouth

½ ounce Amaro Nonino

¼ ounce Fernet-Branca

Glass: rocks

Garnish: large orange wedge

Pour all the ingredients into a glass or shaker. Stir until blended and chilled. Serve up (without ice) in a rocks glass. Peel a large orange wedge over the drink, then drop the peel in the glass.

note

You might also want to add a cherry garnish. If you do, note that this drink's smoothness is such that you'll want a cherry to match its sophistication. Opt for an imported Luxardo maraschino cherry or another fine, artisan-style cocktail cherry.

Lady Lambic

Beer consumption might be dwindling in proportion to the consumption of spirits and wine but, according to the craft brewing industry, the number of women drinking beer is on the uptick.

Beer O'Clock

When making beer cocktails, the ratio of beer to sprits depends on the time of day you're serving the cocktail. If it's for brunch, go three parts beer to one part spirits. If it's an after-dinner drink, go for equal amounts.

Any woman worth her suds also likes a beer cocktail. "If you're going to make a beer cocktail, start with the flavor profile of the beer before you add the spirits," says Lucy Saunders, founder of BeerCook.com and author of beer-related cookbooks, including *Dinner in the Beer Garden.*

Stout often has coffee and chocolate flavors, so it goes well with an Irish cream liqueur or Frangelico. A saison brew, which is unfiltered with a yeasty bite, goes well with Calvados, creating a tart-apple-pie flavor.

Because beer is carbonated, you don't want to shake a beer cocktail; simply pour the spirit into the glass, then add the beer, giving a stir if you need to.

Lift a pint with this refreshing combination of lambic, stout, and crème de cassis.

LADY LAMBIC

1½ ounces crème de cassis

4 ounces Lindemans Cassis lambic

4 ounces stout

Glass: beer flute or pint

Pour the crème de cassis into a beer flute or a pint glass. Add the lambic and stout.

Stop Tequila-ing Me to Smile

Dudes on the street, listen up: We don't owe you a smile, so stop asking us to put on a happy face for your entertainment. And while you're at it, cut out the catcalls and whistles, too.

Women, let's drink to a new day—one when we can walk down the street without being deemed Sweetie or Hon or Baby or Babe by total strangers. And what better drink for a fresh start than a **TEQUILA SUNRISE**?

STOP TEQUILA-ING ME TO SMILE

1½ ounces tequila

3 ounces fresh orange juice

½ ounce grenadine (see recipe on page 206)

Glass: Collins

Garnish: half-moon orange slice and (maraschino) cherry "flag"

Fill a Collins glass with ice. Fill a shaker with ice. Add the tequila and orange juice and shake for 30 seconds. Strain into the prepared glass. Slowly pour in the grenadine, letting it settle to the bottom of the glass. To make the orange "flag" garnish, wrap a half-moon orange slice around a cherry or maraschino cherry, then secure it with a toothpick or cocktail umbrella.

variation

To accentuate the orange juice, add a dropper or dash of your favorite orange bitters.

Lean-In Limoncello

Bartending is in Bridget Albert's blood. Her great-aunt and her great-grandmother had been dressmakers in Italy, but when they immigrated to a small Illinois town called Coal City they realized there was more need for drinks than for dresses. They leaned in, and sometimes over, to watch the bar—back in the day when women weren't bartenders. Albert, author of *Market-Fresh Mixology*, says her family matriarchs were "tough as nails." She adds that her own grandmother, Rosella, grew up while living above the bar and working as a barback. "Her job was to chase out the prostitutes. She was probably eleven years old when she did that."

LEAN-IN LIMONCELLO

Rinds of 12 large lemons

1 750 ml bottle of 100-proof vodka

2 cups simple syrup

½ bar spoon cream of tartar

Glass: cordial

Garnish: none

Add lemon rinds to an infusion jar. Add vodka, and save the vodka bottle. Let rest for three weeks in a dark, cool location. Using a sieve, strain the lemon rinds from the vodka, into a large pitcher. Pour in the simple syrup and cream of tartar, then whisk together. Funnel the mixture back into the original vodka bottle. There will be some leftover so drink or store in another container. Refrigerate. Serve chilled by itself or add it to cocktails.

Bitters-sweet Chocolate

Do you love chocolate? I mean, do you *really love* chocolate? It's okay, it's not your fault. Scientists have proven that craving chocolate is your body's way of asking for a pick-me-up, which chocolate readily supplies: packed with happy-feelings chemicals like phenylethylamine, chocolate releases endorphins and conjures feelings akin to passion.

Whether you have a love affair with chocolate or just an on-again, off-again fling, this not-so-sweet Chocolatini is sure to trigger your pleasure senses.

BITTERS-SWEET CHOCOLATE

1½ ounces vodka

1 teaspoon chocolate extract (see note)

½ teaspoon sweet white vermouth like Dolin Blanc

½ teaspoon simple syrup (see recipe on page 201)

1 dash of Angostura bitters

Glass: Martini or coupe

Garnish: single chocolate chip

Place all ingredients in a glass or shaker filled with ice. Stir until chilled—about 30 to 60 seconds. Strain into martini glass with a single chocolate chip in the bottom.

note

Nielsen-Massey makes a particularly good chocolate extract, but you can also find other chocolate extracts at candy and baking supply stores.

Rethink Pink Drink

A pink cocktail doesn't have to cloy with sweetness or go over the top with fruitiness. It can be just as complex and layered as any other cocktail, and this one is particularly delicious.

RETHINK PINK DRINK

1 ounce Bols genever

1 ounce Jim Beam rye

¾ ounce grenadine (see recipe on page 206)

¼ ounce fresh lemon juice

1 dash of Bar Keep Baked Apple bitters

1 egg white

Glass: coupe

Garnish: Peychaud's bitters

Place genever, rye, grenadine, lemon juice, Bar Keep Baked Apple bitters, and egg white into a cocktail shaker, without ice, and shake vigorously for 1 minute. (This, in bar parlance, is called the "dry shake.") Add ice, and shake vigorously for 1 to 2 minutes more. Strain into a coupe glass, and add 1 dash Peychaud's bitters on top.

Mansplainer — *Antidote* —

Don't you hate it when some guy arches his eyebrows at you before launching into a long-winded explanation of something you *already knew, thank you very much,* because he assumed that because you're female you don't know bunk?

Don't worry—we've got the perfect antidote. Drink this and note the slow but steady dissipation of the inevitable annoyance derived from the ever-predictable, ever-tedious display of man-born arrogance.

MANSPLAINER ANTIDOTE

2 ounces Woodford Reserve Rye

½ ounce Meletti 1870 Bitter Aperitivo liqueur

½ ounce Cocchi Vermouth di Torino
(sweet vermouth)

2 dashes Angostura bitters

4 dashes Scrappy's chocolate bitters

Glass: coupe

Garnish: none

Stir all ingredients with ice until chilled.

The Knockout

Women have been boxing for about as long as boxing has had a history. Even so, for much of that history boxing was outlawed or unsanctioned for women, and it didn't become an official women's Olympic sport until 2012.

What's better for commemorating boxing than a punch? In this case, MILK PUNCH. Chef Claire Menck first learned to make this as a bar manager for river cruise ships that docked in New Orleans. (New Orleans, of course, is known for many different cocktails, including the milk punch.) Claire has spiced up her punch with a garnish of rosemary whipped cream.

THE KNOCKOUT

2 ounces bourbon

2 ounces whole milk

½ ounce simple syrup (optional)
(see recipe on page 201)

Glass: double rocks or Collins if serving on the rocks; coupe if serving straight up

Garnish: 1 cup heavy cream, 1 sprig fresh rosemary, and 1 tablespoon powdered sugar (optional)

First, make the garnish. Add the cream and rosemary sprig to a small saucepan. Over low heat, bring to a bubble, watching closely. As soon as the cream begins to bubble, remove from heat. Let the cream cool to room temperature. Then remove the rosemary sprig and chill the cream. Once it's chilled, whip the cream, with or without the powdered sugar.

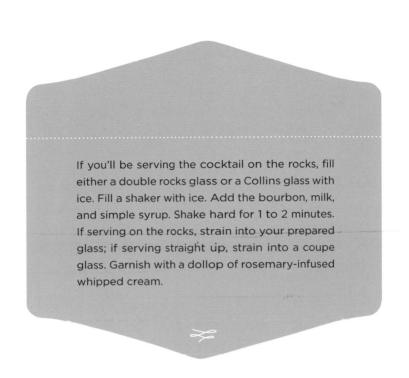

If you'll be serving the cocktail on the rocks, fill either a double rocks glass or a Collins glass with ice. Fill a shaker with ice. Add the bourbon, milk, and simple syrup. Shake hard for 1 to 2 minutes. If serving on the rocks, strain into your prepared glass; if serving straight up, strain into a coupe glass. Garnish with a dollop of rosemary-infused whipped cream.

Then and Now

In 1895, the census revealed that of 55,807 bartenders, a mere 147 were women; that's less than 0.3 percent. At this same time, female physicians numbered around 7,000, or about 5 percent of all doctors. That means there were forty-seven times more women who wielded stethoscopes than there were women who handled shakers. Today, a full 60 percent of bartenders are women, according to the US Bureau of Labor Statistics.

From Zero to Fifty

Back when the National Aeronautics and Space Administration was first established in 1958, there was one type of astronaut: male—a trend that continued at NASA for a full twenty years. Even though the Russians launched into space the first female cosmonaut, Valentina Tereshkova, in 1963, it wasn't until 1977 that NASA even began seeking women to become astronauts. But in 1983, astrophysicist Dr. Sally Ride became the first American woman to fly in space.

Since Sally Ride's launch, forty-nine more American women have also followed her journey beyond the stratosphere. And now, NASA's team of astronauts is made up of just as many women as men—that's right, a full 50 percent.

Just as these rocketeers are blazing a trail in the sky, the NEGRONI is blazing a comeback in bars. Its classic formula is one part gin, one part Campari, and one part sweet vermouth. This recipe offers a twist on the classic by replacing the Campari with Aperol, and calls for a sweet, colorless vermouth.

FROM ZERO TO FIFTY

1½ ounces Nolet's gin

½ ounce Dolin Blanc vermouth

½ ounce Aperol

Glass: rocks if serving on the rocks; Martini or coupe if serving straight up

Garnish: orange twist

If serving on the rocks, fill a rocks glass with ice. Fill a shaker or mixing glass with ice. Add all the ingredients and stir until cold. If serving on the rocks, strain into the prepared rocks glass; if serving straight up, strain into a Martini or coupe glass. Garnish with an orange twist.

PLUS!

Simple Syrups

While many drinks can be rather sophisticated, simple syrups, living up to their name, call for the simple combining of water with sugar.

Most simple syrups have a ratio of one part sugar to one part water, but there are lots of variations. Some bartenders prefer a more syrupy syrup. You can also use fancy sugars—such as Demerara, a raw cane sugar. Brown sugar, honey, and maple syrup are also good choices.

When you're just starting out making your own syrup, begin with the standard 1:1 ratio—then use it in your favorite cocktail to assess how it fares. Too sweet? Not sweet enough? Adjust your ratio to satisfy your palate.

a note about storing:

Pour your cooled syrup into a clean glass jar with an airtight lid. The syrup should keep in the refrigerator for 2 to 4 weeks. Note that many recommend making just the amount of syrup you intend to use, as sometimes crystals can form, or the syrup can take on scents of the refrigerator.

SIMPLE SYRUP

1 cup sugar
1 cup water

The point is to completely dissolve the sugar in the water, which can be done via a few methods. The standard stove-top instructions would have you combine the sugar and water in a small saucepan. Over medium-high heat, whisk the mixture until the sugar is completely dissolved. Or you could boil the water first and then combine it with the sugar, whisking until it's dissolved. You might also stir the sugar and water together in a microwave-safe container with a handle, then heat on high in 1-minute increments, stirring in between, until the sugar is fully dissolved.

Regardless of which method you use, you'll want to let your syrup cool before using.

To make a more syrupy syrup, use 1¼ to 2 cups of sugar per every cup of water.

Flavored Simple Syrups

Of course, "simple" doesn't mean you can't branch out a bit. If you want to get fancy, you can add cinnamon, baking spices, mint, tea, or another pre-flavored syrup. Here are recipes for more complex syrups.

CINNAMON SIMPLE SYRUP

8 to 10 cups of just-made hot simple syrup

1 pound dark brown sugar

7 to 10 cinnamon sticks

Put the brown sugar and cinnamon sticks in a container with at least 2-pint capacity. Pour the hot simple syrup over the sugar and cinnamon. Stir until all the sugar has dissolved and you have a thick and viscous syrup. Let cool before using, at which point you'll want to strain out the cinnamon sticks. If not using right away, leave in the cinnamon sticks; just strain them out before using.

QUICK CINNAMON SIMPLE SYRUP

¼ cup water

¼ cup sugar

½ teaspoon cinnamon

Add the water and sugar to a large glass. Microwave on high for 1 minute. Remove the glass from the microwave and then whisk, stir, or shake until the sugar is completely dissolved. Stir in the cinnamon and let cool for 10 minutes. Strain with a tea strainer before using. Leftover cinnamon syrup adds wonderful flavor to oatmeal, coffee, buttercream frosting, or hot chocolate.

GINGER SIMPLE SYRUP

1½ cups sugar

1 cup water

4 to 5 inches ginger root, peeled and sliced

Put the sugar, water, and ginger root in a medium-sized saucepan. Bring to a simmer over medium-high heat. Simmer for 5 minutes, stirring frequently. Let cool before using.

variation

To make ginger honey syrup, just substitute the sugar with honey.

GRENADINE

Real grenadine syrup, which is made from pomegranate juice, not food coloring and artificial fla-
vorings, is very easy to make.

4 cups fresh pomegranate juice

2 cups mango juice or nectar

1½ cups simple syrup

⅛ teaspoon rose water or elderflower liqueur

Add all the ingredients to a large bowl (mini-
mum 8-cup capacity). Whisk until evenly combined. Remove from the heat and let cool.

HIBISCUS SIMPLE SYRUP

½ cup turbinado or brown sugar

½ cup water

2 hibiscus (or hibiscus-rosehip) tea bags (or 2 teaspoons loose-leaf tea)

Add all the ingredients to a small saucepan. Over medium-high heat, whisk until sugar is dissolved. Remove from the heat, let cool to room temperature. Strain out tea or remove tea bags.

HONEY-ROSEMARY SIMPLE SYRUP

1 cup honey

1 cup water

3 sprigs fresh rosemary

Add all the ingredients to a small saucepan. Stir over low heat until the honey and water are completely combined. Remove from the heat and let cool. Once the syrup has completely cooled, remove the rosemary.

LAVENDER SIMPLE SYRUP

1½ cups sugar

1 cup water

1 tablesppon dried lavender blossoms

Place the sugar, water, and dried lavender blossoms into a small saucepan. Bring to a simmer over medium-high heat. Simmer for 5 minutes. Remove from the heat; let cool. When the syrup is completely cooled, strain out the lavender blossoms.

MINT SIMPLE SYRUP

2 cups water

2 cups sugar

20 to 30 mint leaves (about a large bunch)

Add all the ingredients to a small saucepan. Over medium-high heat, bring the mixture to a boil, stirring constantly. Remove from the heat and let sit at room temperature for 24 hours. Strain out the leaves.

variation

You could also use the mint to infuse bourbon. To do this, place a large bunch—about 20 to 30 leaves—into a clean large mason jar with airtight lid. Cover completely with bourbon. Replace the lid and let it sit for 7 to 10 days. Strain out the mint leaves.

Oleo Saccharum

While oleo saccharum isn't exactly a simple syrup, it's similar to make, and can be used instead of simple syrup. (It's essentially a citrus syrup—called a "citrus cordial"—where citrus juice or peel replaces the water that would be mixed with the sugar.) It's basically a citrus cordial, made with lime or lemon peels and sugar to extract the citrus oils. The following recipe yields 4 ounces, enough for 5 to 16 drinks, depending on your drink recipe. (The recipes in this book call for just ¼ to ½ ounce per Sidecar, ¾ ounce per Daiquiri, or 2 ounces for a bowl of Sylvia's Sword Winter Punch.)

OLEO SACCHARUM

4 ounces white sugar

4 oranges (or blood oranges) or 8 clementines

4 lemons

Place the sugar in a small bowl. Using a vege-table peeler, carefully remove the colored zest—without any white pith—from the oranges and lemons into the bowl. Cover the bowl and let this mixture sit at room temperature for 2 to 24 hours. Before using, strain the zest from the mix-ture, pressing to extract as much liquid as possi-ble. Discard the zest.

Orgeat

Orgeat, an almond-flavored syrup, is the secret ingredient of Mai Tais. Orgeat also tastes great in coffee and coffee-based drinks.

ORGEAT

1 bottle sugar-free almond syrup (about 3¼ cups)

1 cup freshly squeezed orange juice

1½ cups simple syrup

Add all the ingredients to a large bowl (at least 6-cup capacity). Whisk until mixture is evenly combined. Refrigerate until use.

TEA SUGAR SYRUP

1 cup hot water

1 cup sugar

1 tea bag or equivalent of loose-leaf tea

Stir together all ingredients. Let tea infuse according to tea directions and at proper temperature (white, green, black and herbal teas all have different steeping times and temperatures). Remove tea, let cool to room temperature.

GREEN OR WHITE TEA SPIRIT INFUSION

4 tea bags

1 liter spirits

Place tea into spirits. Let sit at room temperature for 24 hours.

BLACK TEA SPIRIT INFUSION

2 tea bags

1 liter spirits

Infuse tea for 4 to 5 hours.

Vanilla Simple Syrup

Vanilla syrup can be used in daiquiris, Irish coffees, and more, and it's ridiculously simple. Just add ½ to 1 teaspoon vanilla extract to 1 cup of simple syrup, to taste.

Six Rules for Creating Creamy — Cocktails —

1. Make all creamy cocktails with half-and-half, not heavy cream. Heavy cream is too cloying.

2. Ice cream can be substituted for ice and half-and-half. Use a small scoop of ice cream, about ¾ cup, for 3 ounces half-and-half.

3. Most cream-based drinks use white crème de cacao, whereas a Brandy Alexander calls for dark crème de cacao.

4. Traditionally, no creamy cocktails receive garnishes except for the Alexander, which calls for a dusting of nutmeg on top. And though it's not traditional, a creative bartender will sometimes top a creamy cocktail with a dollop of whipped cream.

5. Wash out your blender well after making any creamy cocktail. The cream sticks to the blades and will affect the next mixture you blend.

6. The cream drink formula is ¾ ounce liqueur, ¾ ounce crème de cacao (dark or white), and 3 ounces cream. As for liqueur: for the Brandy Alexander use brandy; for the Pink Squirrel use crème de noyaux; for the Velvet Hammer use Cointreau; for the Golden Cadillac use Galliano; for the Banshee use banana liqueur. (As for garnishing the Banshee, adding peanuts, whipped cream, cherries, and chocolate creates a wonderful banana-split feel.)

Help for Hangovers

Long revered for its spicy blend of flavors, the Bloody Mary has been lauded as the perfect "hair of the dog," or hangover cure. Its mix of salt, vegetables, and protein is believed to help restore electrolytes and steady a stomach after a night of indulging. Plus, that nip of vodka might stave off some symptoms.

Here are more suggestions to prevent or relieve a hangover:

WATER, WATER, AND MORE WATER. Drink a glass or two between drinks while you're out imbibing, and then drink two to three glasses before you fall into bed. Since alcohol is a diuretic, it can cause dehydration, which worsens a hangover.

COFFEE. If you are a regular consumer of caffeine, then down a cup or two of coffee. But beware: caffeine, like alcohol, is a diuretic. (Though it also can be noted that coffee's main ingredient is water, so it really isn't that much of a dehydrator.)

SIMPLE CARBS. Remember mom's cure for tummy problems? Nibbling on some whole-grain toast, noshing on a croissant, or just getting a small sandwich into your stomach after a night of drinking can help ease a hangover's ill effects.

FOOD. If you eat while you drink, the food slows the absorption of alcohol and moderates its effects. Certain foods containing sulfur, especially asparagus, can aid liver metabolism. In general, opt for nutrition-rich greens and protein.

ANTI-INFLAMMATORY MEDICATIONS. Ibuprofen and naproxen (Advil and Aleve) are best. Forget acetaminophen or Tylenol, which affect your liver; note too that aspirin slows the metabolism of alcohol, so taking aspirin while drinking can increase intoxication.

BANANAS OR COCONUT WATER. Potassium loss occurs during a night of drinking, so it's a good idea to replenish your body. A nonalcoholic piña colada smoothie in the morning is a rather tasty cure.

GINGER, PEPPERMINT, MILK THISTLE, AND TURMERIC. These herbs have been reported as helpful in easing different symptoms of hangovers. Try steeping them in hot water for a healing cup of tea.

ABSINTHE. Drink this spirit as the last drink of the night. This isn't scientific, but many absinthe lovers swear by it.

Remember that your body takes about an hour to process a single serving of alcohol—twelve ounces of beer, six ounces of wine, or an ounce and a half of booze. One cocktail could contain two or more servings of alcohol. If you're drinking more than your body can process, you are at greater risk for a hangover.

Meet the Mixologists

Say hello to the women who crafted these original recipes for us.

BRIDGET ALBERT developed her techniques and talent tending bar at great establishments, most notably the high-flying Las Vegas resort the Bellagio. The author of *Market-Fresh Mixology: Cocktails for Every Season,* Albert is the master mixologist for Southern Wine & Spirits of Illinois. She is also the director of the Academy of Spirits and Fine Service, a program for bartenders that shares the history of spirits and pre-Prohibition cocktails. Bridget crafted the recipe for LEAN-IN LIMONCELLO.

SUZANNE BRUCE began bartending when she was seventeen at the Boston Sea Party in the suburbs of Chicago. For the last three decades, she's run the bartending program at the College of DuPage in Glen Ellyn, Illinois, during which time she's seen trends come and go. Suzanne crafted recipes for ANARCHY AMARETTO, BUFFY'S STAKE, CLEMENTINE'S COFFEE, CRÈME DE LA FEMME, CURIE ROYALE, DOTTIE COLLINS, THE F WORD, FRIDA KAHLÚA, GIRL POWER SOUR, INVASION OF WOMEN, LITTLE BLACK DRESS, MIND THE (WAGE) GAP, MOTHER'S LITTLE HELPER, MUD MASK, RIZZO, and STOP TEQUILA-ING ME TO SMILE, and also SIX RULES FOR CREATING CREAMY COCKTAILS.

BEVERLY CAMPBELL is co-owner with her husband of the historic Sandshaker in Pensacola Beach, Florida. Their bartending staff is entirely female! Beverly crafted recipes for **MOONSHINE MAMA** and **GROWN-UP GIRL SCOUT.**

A chemist by trade, LESLEY GRACIE is master distiller for William Grant & Sons, where—along with fellow master distiller John Ross—she revolutionized gin with the creation of Hendrick's gin in 1999. She lives in Scotland near the Culzean Castle. While Lesley didn't craft **BEWITCHED** or **GRACE UNDER PRESSURE**, the able mixologists at Hendrick's created them with Lesley in mind.

JUYOUNG KANG was working as a server in Philadelphia when a bartender didn't show up to work a three-hundred-person wedding. The bar manager told her, "You're bartending"—and she has been tending bar ever since. Today she is the lead mixologist at the Delmonico Steakhouse in Las Vegas. Juyoung loves to read, and she loves creating literary cocktails like the one she crafted for this book: **BRONTË'S BREW.**

LYNN HOUSE is the national brand educator for Heaven Hill Brands, the largest family-owned and -operated distilled spirits company in the United States. Lynn has twice been nominated as Best Mixologist by the Jean Banchet Awards committee, Chicago's "local food Oscars." She has also been a national finalist for the 42 Below World Cup finals, the Bacardi Legacy Cocktail Competition, Bombay Sapphire's Most Inspired Bartender Competition, the Esquire Magazine/Benedictine "Alchemist of Our Age" competition, and the Saveur Magazine/Grey Goose Punch Wars. Lynn and her recipes have appeared in many publications, including *Bon Appétit*, the *Chicago Sun-Times*, the *Chicago Tribune*, *Ebony*, *Esquire*, *GQ*, *Imbibe*, *Martha Stewart Living*, *The New York Times*, *Time Out Chicago*, and *The Village Voice*. Lynn crafted the **MONTHLY MEDICINAL**, and Lynn's mixologist best friend Debbi Peek crafted the recipe for **BFF**.

By day, SYDNEY FORGATCH is a recording and mixing engineer for Anthill Studios in St. Louis, Missouri. By night, she enjoys setting drinks on fire at Taha'a Twisted Tiki. Sydney cocrafted the recipes for **JANE AUSTEN'S ZOMBIE!**, **NELLIE BLY-TAI**, and various **SIMPLE SYRUPS**.

SONJA KASSEBAUM, who previously worked in the fields of law and human resources, opened the North Shore Distillery with her husband, Derek, in 2004. Besides running their craft distillery outside of Chicago, she creates all the cocktails for their spirits, and she has a large collection of cocktail books and bitters. She is also the unofficial voice of Ethel, their still—named for her teetotaler granny who sasses off on Twitter @StillEthel. Sonja crafted the recipes for **BESSIE'S GAME CHANGER**, and **TEXAS TWIST**.

Before she tended bar at Rapscallions restaurant in Land O'Lakes, Florida, JULIA MAGER waited tables. After that she moved back home to St. Louis, Missouri, where she worked as a barista and general manager of a coffeehouse before Taha'a Twisted Tiki came calling. She has been the bar manager for this Midwest piece of the tropics ever since. Julia co-crafted the recipes for

JANE AUSTEN'S ZOMBIE!, NELLIE BLY-TAI, and various SIMPLE SYRUPS.

ANNA LEVY MAINS got her start behind the bar because she "talked too much" while waitressing at a restaurant in Texas. After various stints working in marketing for restaurant corporations, she returned to bartending in Oklahoma City, where she met her husband, Drew. In 2012, the couple purchased the In the Raw Sushi Bar where they both bartended; they've since then also bought Knucks and the Rockford Cocktail Den. Anna crafted the recipe for RUTH'S PINK TABOO.

BRIDGET MALONEY originally wanted to go into political science, but a summer spent bartending in her home state of Alaska led her to her true calling. Now she tends bar at Heartwood Provisions in Seattle, Washington. After she attended a Woodford Reserve cocktail competition, she was inspired to investigate whiskey. She was so intrigued by the creativity and the passion she encountered that she ultimately founded the Women Who Love Whiskey club. Within a year this women-centric whiskey organization has grown to more than 130—and there's interest in expanding to other cities. Bridget crafted the recipe for MANSPLAINER ANTIDOTE.

Holding both an MBA and a PhD, J. CLAIRE MENCK was considering law school when she decided to go to culinary school instead. She's now the corporate chef for Emmi Roth USA. She has spent her time as a bartender as well, including as a bar manager for cruise ships. She will always love cocktails, as can be seen in her recipe for BLOODY MARY RICHARDS and THE KNOCKOUT.

While studying design and environmental analysis at Cornell University, JULIA MOMOSE took a job at Rulloff's Restaurant & Bar in Ithaca, New York. First cocktail waitress, then hostess, server, and bar back, she ultimately found her calling as bartender. She conceived some high-concept culinary cocktails while working as bar manager of the Alinea Group's James Beard Award–winning bar The Aviary. Today she is the head bartender at GreenRiver, a bar and restaurant that celebrates the history of Irish-American culture in Chicago. Momose was born and raised in Japan, where her mother entertained with a meticulous appreciation for details. Julia crafted the recipe for LUCILLE'S BALLS.

Chicagoan DEBBI PEEK got her start in the food service industry in high school, and first tended bar at the age of eighteen. While managing the bar at Balina restaurant, she took a class from Southern Wine & Spirits, which inspired her to take her career to the next level; she is now an educator and mixologist in their Florida division. Debbi has also worked at the Pump Room and the Drawing Room, where she became best friends with noted mixologist Lynn House, for whom she honors with the BFF.

Author and bartender JOY PERRINE is one of the best in the business, having tended bar for over fifty years. After growing up in New Jersey, in 1965 she got her start bartending in the Virgin Islands. "My grandmother was a madame and a bootlegger, and my father was a rum runner," she says. After learning her craft in St. Croix, Perrine moved to Louisville, Kentucky. She has spent the last twenty-five-plus years at Equus Restaurant and Jack's Lounge. She is currently working on a follow-up to *The Kentucky*

Bourbon Cocktail Book, which she wrote with Susan Reigler. "As a bartender, you are different things to different people," Perrine says. "You're their mother, their father, their priest, their lawyer, and their psychologist. People tell bartenders things they'd never tell anyone else. And, like Vegas, everything stays here." Joy crafted the recipes for **THE MINT JULEPS**, **DÑA COLADA**, and **MINT SIMPLE SYRUP**.

BENOIT PROVOST is the bar manager at the storied American Bar at The Stafford London hotel. Benoit trained at the Lycée Professionnel catering school in Saint-Nazaire before traveling throughout Europe. He initially joined The Stafford to improve his English; he's now been there twenty-three years and counting. Benoit crafted the **WHITE MOUSE** for Nancy Wake, whom the Nazis could corner but never catch.

When award-winning bartender AMANDA REED started tending bar during her college years in San Francisco, she loved how her interest in travel, people, and culture intersected with food and drink. She went on to become a certified sommelier, and Reed is now the beverage director of Heartwood Provisions in Seattle. Along the way she has worked as general manager at Tavern Law, lead bartender at Michael Mina's RN74, and lead bartender at Bacar Restaurant & Wine Salon. She crafted the recipe for **FLAPPER'S FIREWATER**.

KATIE ROSE grew up on a family farm in Wisconsin before moving to Milwaukee to study at Marquette University. She was pondering a law career when the owner of Burnhearts, a popular bar in the hip Bay View neighborhood, convinced her that, rather than studying for the bar, her calling was behind the bar. Still in Bay View, today she is co-owner of Goodkind, a restaurant and corner tavern where she creates culinary cocktails and where the lines between the kitchen and bar are both blurred and delicious. She crafted the recipe for **BRA BURNER**, **FELIX FIXER**, and **THE INVASION OF WOMEN**.

When she was just a couple weeks shy of her eighteenth birthday, KRISTEN SCHAEFER got her start in the bar of a tiny restaurant outside of San Antonio, Texas—and she's never looked back. After a stint working in upstate New York, she was hired away to Las Vegas, where she helped open the Rhumbar at the Mirage. She was the opening property mixologist for The Cosmopolitan casino before Absolut came calling; she is now their brand ambassador. She is also president of the Las Vegas chapter of the United States Bartenders' Guild. Kristen crafted the recipe for **THE PERFECT CUT**.

CALEY SHOEMAKER didn't create the recipe for **ROSÉ THE RIVETER**, but she distilled the vodka. She started working part-time at Stranahan's Colorado Whiskey, first giving tours on the weekend and then managing the tours and tasting-room program. She went on to become the product administrator, meanwhile apprenticing on the stills. She is now the head distiller at the renowned Hangar One in California.

Few people alive today have been drinking as long as MARCY SKOWRONSKI has been bartending. At the age of ninety, she still works behind the mahogany of the Holler House in Milwaukee, Wisconsin. The bar happens to house the oldest bowling alley in the country, as well as being perhaps the only tavern whose ceiling is festooned with women's brassieres. And, yes, some of the bras on the Holler House ceiling are Marcy's. Mixologist Katie Rose crafted the recipe for **BRA BURNER** in her honor.

KATIE STEWART got her start at a small mom-and-pop bar outside of Chicago, where a longtime bartender named Geri mentored her. Though she went on to work in hot spots in downtown Chicago, she also studied to become an EMT; she was ready to launch that career when she was lured away by the Rocket Bar in Chicago. She has gone on to work at chic bars and restaurants in Austin, Texas, and Knoxville, Tennessee, before coming to Milwaukee, Wisconsin, where you'll find her creating cocktails at The Iron Horse Hotel, the only boutique biker bar hotel in the country. Katie crafted the recipe for **MULTITASKING WOMANHATTAN**.

CHARLOTTE VOISEY is one of the most award-winning bartenders in the world, having won silver at the World Female Bartender Championships in Italy in 2006 and her Punch & Judy earned the best cocktail in the world in 2008 at Tales of the Cocktail. After helming London's Apartment 195, she moved on to become a brand ambassador for William Grant & Sons, where she has twice been awarded best brand ambassador by Tales of the Cocktail, and she also has been recognized by the James Beard Foundation. Today, she is the director for brand advocacy for the company and oversees such brand ambassadors and mixologists who created such drinks as **BEWITCHED** and **GRACE UNDER PRESSURE**.

About the Author

Jeanette Hurt is the award-winning writer and author of eight culinary and drink books, including *The Cheeses of California: A Culinary Travel Guide*, which received the 2010 Mark Twain Award for Best Travel Book, and *The Complete Idiot's Guide to Wine and Food Pairing*. Jeanette has written about spirits, wine, and food for *TheKitchn.com, The Four Seasons Magazine, Wine Enthusiast, Entrepreneur.com, Esquire.com,* and dozens of other publications. When she's not writing, traveling, cooking, or shaking up some concoction with gin, bourbon, or rum, she can usually be found walking along Milwaukee's lakefront with her husband, their son, and their dog.

photo © Kyle Edwards

Index

Selected Titles from Seal Press

The Drinking Diaries: Women Serve Their Stories Straight Up, edited by Caren Osten Gerszberkg and Leah Odze Epstein. $16, 978-1-58005-411-9. Whether it's shame, sober sex, and relapsing, or college drinking, bonding, and comparing the benefits of pot vs. booze, *Drinking Diaries* is a candid look at the pleasures and pains of drinking, and the many ways in which it touches women's lives.

The Women Who Made New York, by Julie Scelfo. $24, 978-1-58005-653-3. Julie Scelfo reveals the untold stories of the phenomenal women who made New York City the cultural epicenter of the world. Paired with striking, contemporary illustrations by artist Hallie Heald, *The Women Who Made New York* offers a visual sensation—one that reinvigorates not just New York City's history but its very identity.

Feminist Activity Book, by Gemma Correll. $12, 978-1-58005-630-4. *The Feminist Activity Book* has everything you need to usher in an era of colorful and intersectional joy. Featuring such activities as Feminist All-Star Trading Cards, Destroy the Page-Triarchy, Sexist Social Media Bingo, and A Feminist ABC, *The Feminist Activity Book* will fuel your feminist rage, remind you to laugh once in awhile, and bring you one step closer to an egalitarian utopia, or whatever.

Mary Jane: The Complete Marijuana Handbook for Women, by Cheri Sicard. $18, 978-1-58005-551-2. *Mary Jane* takes readers on a guided tour through the new world of marijuana, where using pot can be healthy, fun, stylish, and safe. In *Mary Jane,* marijuana expert Cheri Sicard reveals everything women have needed to know but may have been afraid to ask about using cannabis.

Find Seal Press Online
sealpress.com, @sealpress
Facebook | Twitter | Instagram | Tumblr | Pinterest